Data Selves

Data Selves

More-than-Human Perspectives

Deborah Lupton

polity

First published in 2020 by Polity Press

Polity Press
65 Bridge Street
Cambridge CB2 1UR, UK

Polity Press
101 Station Landing
Suite 300
Medford, MA 02155, USA

ISBN-13: 978-1-5095-3641-2
ISBN-13: 978-1-5095-3642-9(pb)

A catalogue record for this book is available from the British Library.

Library of Congress Cataloging-in-Publication Data
Names: Lupton, Deborah, author.
Title: Data selves : more-than-human perspectives / Deborah Lupton.
Description: Cambridge, UK ; Medford, MA : Polity, 2019. | Includes
    bibliographical references and index.
Identifiers: LCCN 2019009946 (print) | LCCN 2019016462 (ebook) | ISBN
    9781509536436 (Epub) | ISBN 9781509536412 (hbk) |
    ISBN 9781509536429 (pbk)
Subjects: LCSH: Information society. | Personal information
    management--Social aspects. | Self-monitoring. | Electronic
    surveillance--Social aspects. | Digital media--Social aspects. | Online
    social networks. | Data protection. | Feminist theory. | Materialism.
Classification: LCC HM851 (ebook) | LCC HM851 .L8638 2019 (print) | DDC
    303.48/33--dc23
LC record available at https://lccn.loc.gov/2019009946

Typeset in 10.5 on 12 Sabon
by Fakenham Prepress Solutions, Fakenham, Norfolk, NR21 8NL
Printed and bound in Great Britain by CPI Group (UK) Ltd, Croydon

For further information on Polity, visit our website: politybooks.com

Contents

1

Introduction

In 2018, as I was writing this book, two major events convulsed the world of personal data politics. The first was the Cambridge Analytica/Facebook scandal in March 2018. News outlets were consumed for weeks with the unfolding story of how over 50 million Facebook users' personal information had allegedly been employed by the data profiling company Cambridge Analytica to manipulate voting behaviour in the presidential election and the British Brexit referendum, both held in 2016. Christopher Wylie, the whistle-blower who had been employed by Cambridge Analytica, claimed that the data analytics company was able to access and use Facebook users' content to provide insights into their deepest thoughts, beliefs, hopes and fears. Many news stories, blog posts and commentaries written about this scandal described the ways in which Facebook and other major internet companies like Google, Amazon and Microsoft collect and use personal information from online interactions and apps, as well as discussing the practices of personal data mining, brokering and profiling companies. These reports commonly used language suggesting that there was a crisis in personal data privacy and security. For example, the British *Daily Mirror* (22 March 2018) published a story with the headline 'Massive Facebook data breach sees "50 million users exposed" in Cambridge

Analytica scandal – are your personal details safe?', while the *Guardian*'s coverage featured headlines such as '"Utterly horrifying": ex-Facebook insider says covert data harvesting was routine' (20 March 2018).

The second major event was the European Union's General Data Protection Regulation (GPDR) legislation, which came into force in May 2018. This legislation was intended to harmonize existing privacy laws across the European Union and replace national data protection rules. It was particularly directed at regulating the ways in which data industries and their clients store and process digitized personal information and rendering the processes more transparent to digital media users (European Commission 2018). The introduction of the GDPR is an important indicator of the strength of concern among governmental bodies, in some countries at least, about the ways in which their citizens' personal data may be exploited and misused by third parties. Internet companies, including the 'Big Five' – Facebook, Apple, Amazon, Microsoft and Google – were forced to make changes to comply with the GDPR. These changes included providing more explicit information to users about how the companies use personal data, and opportunities for users to withhold their consent to their data use and to find their data, rectify inaccuracies and delete their data if they wish. The GDPR only applies to the European Union (EU), but as many internet companies have or seek users in the EU as well as other parts of the world, most have made changes that apply globally.

These events are responses to the intensification of what has been termed the 'datafication' of everyday lives (van Dijck 2014). Datafication enrols an expanding array of digital technologies that are directed at recording aspects of human lives and bodies and rendering them into digitized information. These details are the personal data that are the subject of this book. People's interactions online; their use of mobile and wearable devices, mobile apps and other 'smart' objects; and their movements in sensor-embedded spaces all generate multiple and continual flows of personal data. These data record details about intensely personal actions, habits and preferences, social and intimate relationships, and bodily functions and movements. They can include such attributes as a person's age, gender, date of birth, telephone number, family members, friends and other contacts, email address, home address, educational qualifications, place of work, sexual identity and preferences, ethnicity or race, physical appearance, geolocation, purchasing habits, holiday locations, health status and many more. Internet browsing and search histories using tools such as Google Search document histories of users' interests and preoccupations. Social media sites, including Facebook, Instagram, Twitter and Snapchat, encourage people to continually upload status updates that may include details of their recent activities and social encounters, photographs and videos of themselves and their family members and friends, and information about their hobbies and pastimes, political interests and work life.

The smartphones people carry with them as they move through their days emit constant updates of their physical location using geolocational sensors. The apps that have been uploaded to the phones generate further personal details that are collected by the app developers, often including users' contacts and geolocation. Work-related platforms such as LinkedIn register and display members' educational qualifications and work histories. Content curation and sharing sites, including YouTube and Pinterest, and streaming services such as Netflix and Spotify, record viewing and listening preferences. Messaging apps contain many details about people's relationships and lives as they communicate with others. Electronic health records archive details of visits to doctors, medical tests, medications and therapies. Digitized transport and border security systems record people's travel. Surveillance cameras, facial recognition software and sensors embedded in public spaces document their appearance and movements.

Meanwhile, the use of dating apps and platforms generates details about people's private relationships and sexual preferences. Online customer loyalty reward programs and shopping websites track their purchasing habits. A multitude of apps, software platforms and wearable devices have been designed that encourage people to engage in self-monitoring of their bodies and lives by generating data about themselves, including their heart rate, physical activity, moods, reproductive cycles and sleep patterns. Children can be datafied before they are even born, using digitized foetal ultrasound images and other information about them that can be shared online by their expectant parents. As they enter the school environment, details of children's bodies and activities become further documented through the use of educational and learning analytics software.

The digitized information generated by these entanglements of people with digital devices, apps, sensors and online platforms may be characterized as 'personal data'. Popular representations of these personal data and their futures often lean towards polar extremes. Novel technologies that generate and process personal data are frequently portrayed in news coverage and industry promotional material as almost magical in the possibilities they offer human existence. Many of the positive imaginaries of digital technologies rest on the ideal of surpassing and extending the capabilities and capacities of the fleshly body. It is contended that these devices offer people opportunities to record far greater reams of information about themselves, ready to store and access, than they could using time-honoured analogue technologies (such as pen and paper) or the sensory and memory capabilities of their bodies. Claims are made by digital developers and entrepreneurs that digital devices and software can generate and process information about people that can be used for better self-knowledge and optimization of various aspects of their lives – their health status, longevity, freedom from disability, improved physical fitness, mental wellbeing, greater productivity and so on – in short, to create 'better' humans.

In contrast to these positive and optimistic portrayals, however, a multitude of techno-dystopian visions about the risks and harms of datafication have also received public dissemination in news and other popular cultural forums and by data privacy activists and civil society organizations. As was evident in news coverage of the Cambridge Analytica/ Facebook scandal, public claims are frequently made that personal data offer unprecedented access to people's innermost secrets by unscrupulous and sometimes criminal third parties seeking to uncover and exploit these intimate insights. In many cases, people have little opportunity to discern who is accessing their personal details and how their data are being viewed and used by others. Personal data can be accessed and used without people's knowledge or consent: including illegally by hackers and cybercriminals and via non-malicious data breaches or leakages due to human error.

The Cambridge Analytica/Facebook scandal is only one of a series of highly publicized events that have occurred since 2013 relating to the ways in which digitized information about people was being commodified and exploited by a range of agencies, both legally and illicitly. In 2013, the whistle-blower Edward Snowden released documents demonstrating how the governments of the United States, Canada, the UK, New Zealand and Australia were spying on their citizens as part of the Five Eyes Alliance global mass dataveillance program. Five Eyes intelligence agencies were revealed to be accessing citizens' private emails, phone call data, online searches and other personal data as part of their surveillance activities, and sharing these data with each other. Since then, various other controversial uses of people's personal data by commercial and government organizations as well as data leaking and hacking scandals have occurred: for example, Facebook's and OKCupid's manipulation of information provided to users of their platforms, and massive data breaches and hacks related to personal data held by dating sites; large companies such as Uber, Yahoo, Target, Equifax, the JP Morgan Chase bank and Ebay; and government and healthcare and health insurance organizations. Some of these data breaches or leaks have involved hundreds of millions and even billions of users. These details can be used for identify theft, reputational damage and blackmail. For example, stolen personal data related to dating and sexual relationships have been used for extortion attempts, as in the case of the adultery website Ashley Madison data hack in 2015.

The tension between the contrasting and multiple uses of digitized details about people and the implications for their lives requires sustained examination. In this book, I seek to explore these complexities and identify their sociocultural underpinnings. In my previous book *The Quantified Self: A Sociology of Self-Tracking* (2016b), I discussed the ways in which the emergence of novel modes of generating digital data about humans and their activities and movements has facilitated new understandings about how people learn about and conceptualize their bodies and selves. I developed the concept of 'lively data' in the attempt to characterize and explain the vitality of human–data assemblages (see also Lupton 2017b; 2018b). The first element of the liveliness of personal digital data relates to the ways in which they are generated and what happens thereafter. The intimate information that is continually generated about people as they go about their lives contributes to human–data assemblages that are heterogeneous and dynamic, their character changing as more data points are added and others removed. Digital data may therefore be described as having their own social lives as they circulate in the digital data economy and are purposed and repurposed. These data can continue to be lively even once the human to whom they refer is dead. Second, digital data constitute forms of knowledge about human (and nonhuman) life itself: the attributes of being alive. Third, personal digital data have impacts on people's lives, shaping the decisions and actions that people make for themselves, and those that others make on their behalf. Finally, personal digital data are forms of human livelihoods, contributing to the commodification of information as part of the digital data economy.

Data Selves offers a complementary discussion to *The Quantified Self* of how personal digitized information – derived not only from self-tracking activities but also from a wide variety of humans' engagements with digital technologies – are conceptualized, used and interpreted as part of subjectivity, embodiment and social relations. Working and thinking particularly with perspectives from scholarship in feminist new materialism, I acknowledge the importance of paying attention to practices, affects and sensory and other embodied experiences, as well as discourses, imaginaries and ideas, in identifying the ways in which people make and enact data, and data make and enact people. In so doing, I seek to explore the onto-ethico-epistemiological (Barad 2014) dimensions of living with and through our lively data, generating our 'data selves'. This approach recognizes that understandings, knowledges and ethical positions are always entangled and mutually generative.

Dataveillance and personal data commodification

Much of the digitized information about humans that is currently collected and processed can be used for dataveillance (Raley 2013; van Dijck 2014), or the watching and monitoring of people using their personal data. Dataveillance can be employed for a wide variety of purposes. It is undertaken at the personal or interpersonal level, involving voluntary self-surveillance or the consensual surveillance of others. In some cases, people have been informed about how their personal data may be used and have agreed to terms and conditions and privacy policies concerning third-party use. They may choose to actively collect digitized information about themselves using devices and software specifically designed for this purpose. They can take the opportunity to view their personal information, reflect on its meaning and use it to improve their lives, contribute to their memories or achieve self-knowledge. They can choose to connect with other people online, consensually sharing and responding to personal details as part of social networks and friendships. People can also sometimes review data about themselves collected by other actors, such as social media metrics, employee dashboards, educational outcomes, medical records and so on.

However, people's digitized details can also be used by third parties to betray, discipline, marginalize or even punish them, and to deny them rights and opportunities. Dataveillance can operate at the organizational level, conducted by actors such as commercial enterprises, government intelligence, security and policing agencies, social security agencies, transport organizations, workplaces, educational institutions and many more. Researchers have identified 'function creep', or the ways in which datafication technologies and personal datasets have become dispersed into and used in different domains well beyond their original purpose (Timmermans et al. 2010; Kitchin 2014; Lupton 2016a; 2016b). As I outlined in *The Quantified Self*, there are many ways in which people may be pushed or even coerced into generating and sharing digitized information about themselves. Some businesses now offer reward schemes that provide financial or other compensation to people who share their personal data with them. Retailers' customer loyalty schemes collect information about people's purchasing habits, and some companies encourage people to upload their physical activity data generated by wearable devices. Employers now often encourage their employees to take up self-tracking as part of workplace wellness programmes, staff competitions and challenges or productivity campaigns, or compel workers to use software and sensors to monitor their movements and engagements online. Schools may require their students to sign up to apps or platforms in which their learning is tracked, or to use physical activity monitoring equipment in physical education lessons. Health and life insurance companies have begun to encourage their customers to engage in health- and fitness-related self-tracking using apps or wearable devices, and to share their data with the companies, so that individualized premiums can be calculated based on this information. Car insurers offer similar schemes for clients, in exchange for digital data on their driving habits. Social security and law enforcement agencies may demand that the people in their remit share personal data such as their income and physical location with them.

Underpinning these initiatives is the notion that personal digitized information is valuable. In the contemporary information economy – or what Zuboff (2015) calls 'surveillance capitalism' – personal data, like human tissue, blood or cells, have become commercial commodities, attracting a form of biovalue that can be exploited for profit by a diverse range of actors (Ebeling 2016; Lupton 2016b). These 'small data' on individuals accumulate into larger datasets and become 'big data' (Kitchin 2014; Zuboff 2015). Surveillance capitalism is built on an emergent logic of accumulation that depends on the continual collection of data and their extraction and analysis to generate revenue (Fuchs 2014; Zuboff 2015; Sadowski 2019). Personal data can be used by an app, device or platform developer to be sold to third parties such as advertisers and data-broking and -profiling companies, or to better market their product to targeted audiences. The vast profits of internet empires Google and Facebook depend on the monetization of personal data. A secondary industry of data miners, harvesters and brokers has sprung up, in which data about people are traded and brought together to create profiles or to use in algorithm decision-making processes. People's digitized information is used to optimize systems, model probabilities and train artificial intelligence software (Andrejevic 2013; O'Neil 2016; Sadowski 2019). Government agencies or researchers may use some of these data for managerial or research purposes. There is even an industry that seeks to preserve and exploit the 'digital assets' of dead people (Arnold et al. 2017; Öhman and Floridi 2018).

Personal data can be further used in digitized systems that reproduce or set social norms of behaviour and discipline and regulate citizens. China's integrated facial recognition 'Sharp Eyes' software and its 'Social Credit' system that bring together a range of personal data provide a salutary example of how far governments may go in engaging in dataveillance of their citizens, with major implications for their rights, freedoms and opportunities. Dataveillance can be very difficult to identify, particularly when it involves hidden sensors, using software in which the terms and conditions and privacy policies are absent or not well explained; algorithmic decision-making which lacks transparency; or illicit access. The imputed scientific neutrality of digital data and digitized processing systems lends credence to these forms of establishing and policing social norms and behaviours, and they can therefore be hard to challenge, even when the decisions that these forms of data processing make about people are inaccurate or incomplete (Pasquale 2015; Ananny and Crawford 2016).

In response to the expansion of datafication and dataveillance, academic researchers and privacy advocates have begun to identify the ways in which the use of automated decision-making and data profiling software can have significant repercussions for people's life chances and opportunities. A rapidly developing body of literature in critical data studies focuses on elements of personal data use, particularly emphasizing the third-party use of personal data and the ways in which dataveillance takes place and potentially harms or marginalizes people. The term 'data harm' is now used by some researchers to describe the manifold ways in which people's digital data can be used against them (see, for example, the list of data harms collected by Redden and Brand 2019), while other scholars refer to 'data power' (Kennedy and Moss 2015) and 'metric power' (Beer 2017) to gesture towards the authority and agency of digital data and algorithmic processing to offer scientific objectivity and accuracy even while they privilege some individuals and social groups over others and reward certain types of behaviour.

Researchers interested in internet and app privacy issues have drawn attention to the potential risks and harms posed by the ever-expanding amounts of personal data that are generated and stored in digital archives. A growing number of researchers have identified the loss of control that publics have over their personal data. For example, they have demonstrated how mobile apps can transmit users' personal data to dozens of third parties (Brandtzaeg et al. 2018) and how public WiFi networks, sensor-embedded public spaces and smartphones track people's location (Leszczynski 2015). Personal data can be harvested and sold for profit by the companies that offer the devices and software for self-tracking (Barcena et al. 2014). Data collected by health and fitness-tracking apps and wearable devices may be inadvertently breached or leaked, or hackers and cybercriminals may deliberately access the data illegally. These data are valuable on the black market, used for such activities as fraudulent health insurance claims and obtaining drugs or medical devices (Wolff et al. 2016).

The implications of personal data exploitation for social justice and civil rights have also been identified. The use of personal data by data companies for profiling, sorting and prediction is increasingly common (Rosenblat et al. 2014; Ebeling 2016; Kennedy 2016). The expanding employment of automated decision-making software has led to important decisions being made about people using the data about them that can be found online, harvested and algorithmically manipulated. For example, the predictions that are made by data analytics can result in predictive privacy harms, in which people may be discriminated against simply because they are categorized within certain social groups based on digitized information about them. This can affect people's access to healthcare, credit, insurance, social security, educational institutions, travel and employment options and render them vulnerable to unfair targeting by policing and security agencies (Crawford and Schultz 2014; Redden and Brand 2019).

High-profile books such as *The Black Box Society* (Pasquale 2015), *Weapons of Math Destruction* (O'Neil 2016), *Algorithms of Oppression* (Noble 2018) and *Automating Inequality* (Eubanks 2018) have outlined the ways in which algorithmic decision-making can work to marginalize and discriminate against already marginalized social groups in Western countries, including people living in poverty and non-white people, exacerbating social problems such as socio-economic inequalities, racism and sexism. Concerns have consequently been raised by privacy, civil rights and ethics organizations and legal scholars about invasions of personal privacy incurred by digital data harvesting and analytics practices (Tene and Polonetsky 2013a; Crawford and Schultz 2014; Nuffield Council on Bioethics 2015).

Other commentators have discussed the commercialization of digitized personal information, and drawn attention to the ways in which these details may be used for the financial benefit of others (Andrejevic 2014; Lupton 2015b; Cate 2016). Political issues concerning data ownership are also emerging. Critical data scholars have identified the asymmetries in the access of citizens to digital datasets (including their personal data) and that of government and commercial entities (Andrejevic 2013; Crawford and Schultz 2014). Whereas heightened visibility in digitized databases can cause data harms, lack of visibility can also be a significant problem. The data collected about people are often inaccurate or missing, and this can particularly affect homeless, poor or otherwise marginalized people whose information is not routinely collected because they lack access to health and social services or to online technologies. For example, medical datasets in the United States often have limited or incomplete health information of people who have low access to healthcare services. These people tend to be those who are already disadvantaged and experience poorer health. Lack of information about them exacerbates their problems with receiving adequate healthcare, as their needs are not adequately documented (Ferryman and Winn 2018).

In Australia, indigenous advocates have called for indigenous data sovereignty, arguing that Aboriginal and Torres Strait Islander people are subjected to data collection by others that has worked to intensify their stigmatization and limit their autonomy. In contrast, too little information has been generated about the social, cultural, spatial and political complexities of their lived experiences. These advocates have argued that more of this kind of data is needed to give indigenous people a voice and greater control over policy decisions and service delivery, allowing them to better set the agenda concerning the type of information about them that is collected and used (Walter 2018).

In a different but related field of research, scholars interested in information ethics have begun to call for a specific field of enquiry that focuses on the moral problems associated with the collection and use of personal data. Trust and transparency are integral issues for data ethicists. They have questioned the lack of knowledge and control that people have over how their personal information is collected and used by third parties, challenges to people's free will by manipulation of their decision-making, and restrictions to opportunities that processing of their data may promote (Zwitter 2014; Danaher 2016; Floridi and Taddeo 2016). Outside the academy, civil society organizations have advocated for greater regulation of agencies' use of personal data and for datasets to be rendered more open to the public.

Human–data assemblages

These are important issues concerning personal data that require identification and detailed discussion, some of which is provided in further detail in the pages of this book. My main focus, however, is somewhat different. I argue that concepts of selfhood, identity and embodiment and how they are enacted with digital technologies as part of everyday life are central to understanding personal data experiences. As the title *Data Selves* suggests, I take an approach that views people and their data as inextricably entangled in human–data assemblages. These assemblages are configured via interactions of humans with other humans, devices and software, as well as the multitude of other things and spaces they encounter as they move through their lives.

The phenomenon of personal digital data poses a challenge at an ontological level. Personal data blur and challenge many of the binary oppositions and cultural boundaries that dominate in contemporary Western societies. Personal data are both private and public. They could be considered to be owned by, and part of, the people who have generated them, but these details are also accessed and used by a multitude of other actors and agencies. At a deeper level, personal data challenge the ontological boundaries between the binary oppositions of Self/Other, nature/culture, human/nonhuman and living/dead. Discussions of how digital data about and for people are incorporated into everyday lives must therefore grapple with the problem of how we conceptualize the idea of 'the human' and 'life' in relation to the digital data that are generated by and for humans. Because digital data are associated with nonhuman entities such as digital devices and software, and because they are often viewed as non-material entities, they are often dehumanized and dematerialized in discourses. The oft-used term 'big data', for example, tends to portray large digital datasets as depersonalized and anonymous, even though these datasets often consist of very intimate and sensitive details about people and their lives. Alternatively, explanations of how people collect and make sense of their own data are often reduced to individualized models of cognition or behavioural psychology, removing the sociocultural, sensory and affective dimensions of how people generate and respond to these details about themselves.

Recent existential philosophical theories of human experience in the digital media world have reflected on the challenges faced by people when they engage with their personal data. For example, Amanda Lagerkvist (2017) examines what she describes as the 'thrownness of digital human existence'. She argues that rather than the 'user', a better term for the individual negotiating digital technologies and media is that of the 'exister', who is seeking meaning and existential security. Lagerkvist calls for an emphasis on the insecurities and struggles in which people engage when encountering new digital technologies and a rapidly changing world. She characterizes this exister subject as vulnerable in her or his attempts to make sense of the novelty of digital lifeworlds. Lagerkvist argues that the exister is a relational being, both with other humans and with nonhumans. The pervasiveness of digital media results in people engaging in profound practices of being. While the digital technologies they use may be viewed as mundane elements of everyday life, they create opportunities for self-reflection, meaning making and the quest for existential security.

One element of this quest, Lagerkvist suggests, is confronting the new potential for personal details to be preserved, distributed in manifold ways and reconfigured and repurposed online. She contends that the distributed nature of people's personal digital assemblages invokes anxiety about how to keep track of these details and who is accessing them, as well as more profoundly about their identities. People know that these assemblages exist, but often cannot access them or know where they exist, and feel vulnerable about the ways in which these details may be used against them or illegally accessed. This raises questions about how people come to terms with their digitally distributed selves as part of existential being. According to Lagerkvist, it is in this way that the mundane everydayness of digital life is also momentous and extraordinary.

I agree with Lagerkvist's characterization of digital life as both momentous and extraordinary. In this book, I address some of these issues as they relate to personal digitized information, primarily drawing on feminist new materialism theoretical perspectives. My concern is with the relationships of humans with non-organic things – digital technologies in particular – and how these engagements are infused with vitalities and vibrancies. I use the term 'more-than-human' to acknowledge that human bodies/selves are always already distributed phenomena, interembodied with other humans and with nonhumans, multiple and open to the world. Adopting this approach, human–data assemblages can be viewed as ever-changing forms of lively materialities. A feminist new materialism perspective can draw attention to their potentialities, challenges and limitations, as humans learn to live with and through them.

Feminist new materialism is a branch of new materialism (also sometimes referred to as sociomaterialism), a diverse range of theoretical perspectives interested in the ways in which humans and nonhumans come together. In new materialism, the poststructuralist emphasis on language, discourse and symbolic representation is enhanced by a turn towards the material: particularly human embodied practices and interactions with objects, space and place. Understanding how agencies are generated and the capacities they create is a central interest in feminist new materialism. Key scholars such as Donna Haraway, Karen Barad, Jane Bennett and Rosi Braidotti emphasize the micro-politics of embodied encounters of humans with nonhumans, and the ways in which all agents work together to generate agential capacities that impel and shape human action.

Feminist new materialist scholars have called for taking an approach Braidotti (2018) terms 'critical posthumanities', in which the concept of human exceptionalism is done away with. This more-than-human approach sees human bodies as extending beyond their fleshly envelopes into the physical environment, while the environment likewise colonizes human bodies. Spinoza's conceptualization of affect as a relational force is important in feminist new materialism scholarship. From the Spinozian view, affect is understood as a force that is generated with and from assemblages of humans and nonhumans that has the capacity to affect and be affected. The writings of Deleuze and Guattari are very influential, particularly their concepts of the affective force of relations between things in assemblages and the lines of flight that offer paths for doing and thinking otherwise. Latour's actor-network approach has also been taken up by feminist new materialism scholars to emphasize the agencies generated by assemblages of humans and nonhumans.

The question of how we understand and live with our digital data is, at heart, a biopolitical issue. Biopolitics involves bodies and ways of living and how they are imbricated within networks and relationships of power. If we view personal digital data as manifestations of vitality, as recording, monitoring and influencing human lives, generating biovalue and indeed as essentially part of humans, then they become part of the domain of biopolitics. Michel Foucault's scholarship has been particularly influential in addressing biopolitics and the related concept of biopower.

Foucault's main focus was on the ways in which human life is managed, regulated, ordered and disciplined via modes of power exerted by the state and dominant institutions (such as the medical clinic and the criminal justice system) (Foucault 1979; 2008). His work, published in a pre-digital age, drew attention to the role of information about people, noted and stored in non-digital formats such as paper journals or records, in generating norms of human life against which people or groups could be compared and assessed as part of governing populations. It is valuable in drawing attention to the intersections between institutional and managerial authority and technologies of monitoring, measuring and comparing people and creating sets of information about them.

As Foucault contended, biopower is productive: it brings people and social groups into new fields of visibility by generating information about them which can be used to order and control them. Biopower fosters and brings life into being. It is a soft form of power, therefore, that relies less on coercion and obvious displays of authority and discipline than on dispersed networks of knowledge and management that seek to identify and optimize human potential. The feminist new materialism perspective extends Foucauldian theory on biopolitics by focusing to a greater extent on how all actors – human and nonhuman – potentially have agency, but always with and through other actors. Working together, actors create affective forces and agential capacities for feeling, sensing, learning or doing.

While feminist new materialism scholarship has been strongly influenced by these theorists, a major point of difference is its emphasis on vitalities and vibrancies that are distributed among and between humans and nonhumans when they assemble. This approach is sometimes referred to as 'agential materialism' or 'vital materialism', due to feminist new materialism's focus on the relational and lively dimensions of the agencies that are generated by human–nonhuman assemblages. Because of their feminist standpoint, feminist new materialism scholars work to uncover the gendered dimensions of the more-than-human world. They are also concerned with other political issues and relations of power, especially those relating to the environment and the

Anthropocene. Feminist new materialists celebrate the renewal and liveliness of the capacities that human–nonhuman assemblages generate at the same time as identifying the ways in which these capacities can be closed off or limit the freedoms and potentials of some people or social groups or generate harm for the more-than-human world, as in environmental degradation, global warming, species extinction, pollution and climate change. Indigenous and First Nations philosophies have begun to play an important role in contributing to feminist new materialism thinking on the vitalities and ethics of more-than-human worlds.

Thus far, few feminist new materialism scholars have turned their attention to issues of the engagements of humans with contemporary digital technologies and the data that are generated from these engagements. Yet I argue that bringing together the insights offered in their scholarship has much to offer a nuanced analysis of the onto-ethico-epistemologies of human–data assemblages. Making sense of personal data requires developing practices that can manage and interpret lively data to make them useful and knowable. Digital data and humans can potentially learn from each other as they come together. But humans may find themselves asking to what extent their data speak for them, how they might betray them, and how their data are different from other elements of their embodiment and selfhood. Thinking with a feminist new materialist theoretical approach can help to surface some of these complex relationships. They can help us become sensitized to the vulnerabilities as well as the beneficial capacities of human–data assemblages, and the associated ethics of care that are integral to how we can best live with our data selves.

A key preoccupation of my discussions in this book is the indeterminacy of the distinctions between human and nonhuman that human–data assemblages enact. I suggest that not only do human–data assemblages configure and materialize certain dimensions of human embodiment and selfhood, they also have material effects on humans in recursive ways. This approach is underpinned by the understanding that when digital data come together with humans and other nonhuman actors, they generate dynamic human–nonhuman assemblages that create specific agential capacities that are distributed between the humans and nonhumans involved. I seek to provide some insights into how to conceptualize and understand how people live with, in and through digital data about themselves: how they make sense of and use their data and what they know about who else makes use of this information.

One focus of this book is identifying the sociotechnical imaginaries that articulate the promises and perils of the expansion of human datafication and dataveillance technologies in popular culture. Jasanoff (2015) describes sociotechnical imaginaries as promotional, public and positive, supportive of new technologies. My use of the term, however, incorporates the ways in which negative as well as positive visions are generated and performed in both public and private forums. I argued that personal data imaginaries are suffused with affect, suggesting their attractive and enchanting but also disturbing and discomforting elements.

Directing attention to the ways in which the affordances of human bodies come together with those of digital technologies is also a central feature of my analysis of data selves. Affordance is a term that is often used in media studies to describe the opportunities for action that digital technologies invite, allow, demand, close off or refuse to human users (Davis and Chouinard 2016). Here, I expand this concept to include a more-than-human consideration of the ways in which the enfleshed affordances of human bodies – their sensory perceptions, thoughts, memories, desires, imaginings, physical movements and feelings – come together with digital technologies in a variety of ways that may or may not fulfil their promised uses.

In what follows, I examine the interplay of human and nonhuman affordances associated with digital technologies – devices, software and the digital data they generate – and the agential capacities that are opened up or closed off as these things assemble. I ponder the questions of who benefits from these agential capacities, and in whose interests they operate. Here again, affective forces are central to the engagements of humans with these nonhuman things and the capacities that are generated by their gatherings. I address how human–data assemblages can generate agential capacities that empower and vitalize actors in the assemblage; but can also expose them to vulnerabilities and harms.

This approach recognizes the entanglements of personal digital data assemblages with human action, reaction and understanding of the world. Personal digital data assemblages are partly comprised of information about human action, but their materializations are also the products of human action, and these materializations can influence future human action. While digital data assemblages are often conceptualized as immaterial, invisible and intangible, I contend that they are things that are generated in and through material devices (smartphones, computers, sensors), stored in material archives (data repositories), materialized in a range of formats that invite human sensory responses and have material effects on human bodies (documenting and having recursive effects on human flesh). The primary analytical focus is understanding what personal data assemblages allow bodies to do, and how they come to matter in people's lives.

Feminist new materialism also calls into question and problematizes how we might define and materialize personal data. While the literatures on datafication and dataveillance tend to assume that personal data are digital artefacts that are primarily materialized in two-dimensional visual formats as the outcomes of humans' encounters with digital technologies, an emergent body of scholarship in what has been termed 'posthuman' or 'post-qualitative' inquiry (Lather and St. Pierre 2013; MacLure 2013) contends that data about humans can be any kind of matter, both organic and inorganic. Human flesh, bones, tissue, blood, breath, sweat or tears; human sensory and affective responses and reactions; objects that people use as part of their mundane routines; or artworks and creative writing outputs, for example, are among the materializations of and participants in human experience that can be viewed and treated analytically as 'data' (Koro-Ljungberg et al. 2017; Taylor et al. 2018).

Drawing on this perspective, I argue that examining the multitude of media (loosely defined) that are used to represent personal data, including arts-based and three-dimensional approaches, is one way of working towards a different way of thinking about their onto-ethico-epistemological aspects. Expanding the definition of what materials can be treated as personal data works to highlight the performative, embodied, multisensory, affective and agential dimensions of human–data assemblages. Not only does this perspective acknowledge the more-than-human worlds of personal data, it also highlights the more-than-digital dimensions of these assemblages.

In this book, I take up calls by Barad (in Dolphijn and Van der Tuin 2012) and Braidotti (2018) for a critical posthuman studies that incorporates an affirmative ethics. For Braidotti (2018), the mutable and distributed nature of human agency offers a politics that is able to challenge current fears and preoccupations. Cartographies of power relations and their associated entitlements, agencies and capacities can provide detailed ways of thinking through and with political practices and subjectivities. They help to think differently about figurations of human action, belief and practice; their implications, boundaries and limitations; and how new modes of being and acting can be configured and political change effected.

Central to my argument is that in the face of the continuing depersonalization and dehumanization of details about people's bodies and lives that have been rendered into digital data, a new onto-ethico-epistemological position should be developed that reinvests human–data assemblages with different meanings and reconceptualizes what we mean by 'personal data' – and indeed, how we think about and treat our 'data selves'. In so doing, we can begin to think more seriously and deeply about what is at stake when human–data assemblages are depersonalized and dehumanized. If these new ways of thinking are taken up, they have a significance that goes to the core of selfhood, social relations and embodiment as they are enacted in more-than-human worlds.

Structure of the book

In making my argument in the pages of this book, I seek to engage in what Barad (2007) refers to as 'diffractive methodology', which attempts to work with different bodies of research and theory to generate new insights. As she notes, it is the diffractive patterns of resonances and dissonances that make entanglements of matter and meaning visible. For Barad, diffractive thinking goes beyond critique to ethical engagements, involving reading insights through one another:

'Diffractive readings bring inventive provocations; they are good to think with' (Barad in Dolphijn and Van der Tuin 2012: 50). In the spirit of a diffractive approach, this book's content is intentionally interdisciplinary and eclectic. While I work principally with feminist new materialism theory, relevant perspectives offered from scholarship in the anthropology of material culture, digital sociology, media studies, internet studies, cultural studies, information studies, archival studies, human–computer interaction studies, education, archaeology and cultural geography are also included.

Chapter 2 provides an overview of these perspectives and begins to explore how they might be taken up to theorize the more-than-human worlds of human–data assemblages. In chapter 3, I address the ways in which personal data as a phenomenon is materialized in words, images and three-dimensional representations, including provocations and interventions from design- and arts-based approaches that offer alternative ways of thinking about personal data. In chapters 4 and 5, I draw on empirical material from several research projects I have conducted since 2015 to provide insights into how people conceptualize and live their personal data. (Details of these projects are provided in the Appendix.) Chapter 4 discusses how people enact and make sense of their personal data and identifies the relational connections, affective forces and agential capacities generated by doing data. Chapter 5 reviews the ways in which the tension between the sharing ethos of participatory digital media and the dystopian imaginaries that circulate concerning the 'internet knowing too much' about people are dealt with in everyday data concepts and practices. In the Final Thoughts section, I present my vision for how a new ethics of caring about and living with our data selves might be developed.

2

More-than-Human Perspectives

This chapter provides an overview of what I see as the key concepts and perspectives offered in feminist new materialism theory and other sociocultural areas of scholarship that can contribute to theorizing and researching personal data. I focus in particular on how this scholarship may be employed to conceptualize the vitalities, affective forces and agencies of human–data assemblages.

More-than-human vitalities

New materialisms theory has brought to the fore major questions concerning not only how to conceptualize the human, but also the related issue of how to define the boundaries between living and non-living entities. Recent sociocultural theory has noted that definitions of 'life' are constantly subject to reconfigurings. Gender and cultural studies scholars Jami Weinstein and Claire Colebrook (2017) contend that critically reframing and rethinking the notion of life should be the key problematic of critical theory. They adopt the phrase 'critical life studies' to encapsulate the various perspectives and positions that address the questions of what is life, how human life may differ from other forms of life, how we come to know life, and which lives matter.

This is a new form of vitalism that requires thinking beyond the human conditions of existence, decentring and complicating the human form of vitality – 'delving into the inchoate labyrinth of life and posing forbidden questions' (Weinstein and Colebrook 2017: 5).

One term that is often employed to describe humans' entanglements with things such as digital technologies is 'posthuman'. Confusingly, this term has several different definitions. Posthuman is often used to denote a state in which humans transcend the limits of life in some way, and therefore, are beyond the human (Colebrook and Weinstein 2017). This latter version of posthumanism was particularly evident in early discussions of the possibilities of 'cyberspace' following the emergence of personal computing and the internet late last century (Lupton 1995). For Katherine Hayles (2008; 2012), posthumanism involves the distributing of the human into nonhuman objects such as digital technologies. Human memory, for example, can be supplemented and extended by digital recording and archiving of details of people's lives. Posthuman can also refer to the conquering of death or other physical failings of the body, such as disease or disability (also referred to as transhuman). The term is also sometimes used to describe how Earth might be characterized 'after humans': that is, when human life has been extinguished (Colebrook and Weinstein 2017). Weinstein and Colebrook suggest a shift in terminology from 'posthuman' to 'posthumous'. They argue that the term 'posthumous' acknowledges the vitality that exists in many kinds of human and nonhuman assemblages and thinking beyond the human conditions of existence.

I prefer to use the term 'more-than-human', as I see this phrase as encapsulating the inextricable entanglement of humans with nonhumans, to the point that 'the human' always already incorporates 'the nonhuman', and vice versa. As such, this perspective can be characterized as an animist cosmology. 'Animism' is a term that is used in sociocultural theory to refer to the attribution of life, human characteristics or spirituality to phenomena that are otherwise culturally considered non-living or nonhuman (such as rocks, rivers, plants, technologies, houses and so on). It is a relational perspective that views humans and nonhumans as interconnected and trans-agential. Life, or vitality, is seen as not possessed by any individual actor, but rather as constantly generated with and through interactions (Bennett 2009; Chen 2012; Jensen and Blok 2013).

This is quite a radical onto-ethico-epistemological position, as it directly challenges dominant Western beliefs about the unique qualities of humans compared with other living things, and the autonomy and individuation of human bodies/selves that these beliefs espouse. This Western belief system, however, is a relatively recent and localized worldview. As historians and anthropologists have identified, animist cosmologies are historically and culturally contingent. They have antecedents in indigenous and pre-modern cosmologies. People in pre-modern Western cultures held animist cosmologies that blurred binaries between Self and Other, subject and object, humans and animals, culture and nature. Superstition and magical beliefs, blended with religious beliefs, served to animate the more-than-human worlds in which people conducted their everyday lives (Szerszynski 2008; Cameron 2010).

Many indigenous worldviews have traditionally incorporated the nonhuman world into understandings of human ontologies and spiritualities (Jones and Hoskins 2016). The indigenous Australian concept of 'Country', for example, positions the land as a 'living and life-giving nexus of energy/matter', incorporating humans and their ancestors as well as nonhumans (Ravenscroft 2018: 361). In indigenous North American narratives about the sweetgrass plant, this organism is depicted as an intermediary between humans and the land, operating as a teacher in instructing humans about their connectedness to humans and nonhumans via sensory properties such as its scent, texture and literal rootedness in the earth. These relational connections often operate at the more-than-representational level, in which sensory embodied experiences relationally connect humans with nonhumans, generating an ethics of engagement with more-than-human worlds (Cariou 2018).

Contemporary cultures in developed societies also sometimes incorporate strongly animist ontologies. For example, Japanese culture is influenced by the legacy of Shinto philosophies and folkloric traditions, which ignore boundaries between humans and nonhumans and see all actors as invested with spirits and contributing to collective life (Jensen and Blok 2013). In what has been described as 'techno-animism' (Allison 2006: 13), new technologies are considered as possessing vital forces, where the boundaries between object and life are constantly blurred. Technoanimism is a central affective and agential force in Japanese commodity culture. People develop companionate relationships with technological objects like machines, such as robots or toys, in ways that are quite different from Western relational modes (Allison 2006; Jensen and Blok 2013).

The development of scientific thinking and industrial capitalism in modern Western societies led to privileging worldviews that sought to more stringently define and police the boundaries between humans and nonhumans and nature and culture (Szerszynski 2008). The Cartesian dualism between mind and body was also established as a phenomenon of modernity (Hornborg 2006). It is debatable, however, to what extent Western cultures have rejected animist ontologies outright. Bruno Latour (1993) famously argues that 'we have never been modern', as new hybrid more-than-human entities are continually emerging that challenge these boundaries. His actor-network theory attempts to demonstrate the relational connections between human and nonhuman actors.

Feminist new materialism theory also draws on concepts of relational agency and vital materialism to position vitalities and agencies as distributed over different actors that come together to generate novel emergent forms. Among feminist new materialism scholars, Donna Haraway stands out as a theorist who has discussed the blurred boundaries between humans and digital technologies for several decades. Her writings on the figure of the cyborg (e.g., Haraway 1991; 1995; Bhavnani and Haraway 1994) have been influential in conceptualizing human and computer technological encounters. In this work, Haraway drew attention to the idea that human ontologies must be understood as multiple and dynamic rather than fixed and essential (Bhavnani and Haraway 1994). Haraway's (2003) later concept of 'companion species' described the relationships that humans have not only with other animal species but also with technologies. She argued that humans are companion species with the nonhumans alongside which they live and engage, each species learning from and influencing the other: co-evolving. Haraway (2015b) has referred to companion species as 'post-cyborg entities', acknowledging the development of her thinking since her original cyborg exegesis.

Haraway's more-than-human approach is even more radical in her recent work. She now prefers to reject the term posthuman altogether. She claims that the prefix 'post' tends to assume that the 'human' part remains, and that a distinction can be made between humans and nonhumans. She now positions humans metaphorically as compost, intertwined with other living and nonhuman entities in a rich, dense matter in which the boundaries between objects cannot be distinguished, so that 'we make with, and we become with each other' (Franklin and Haraway 2017: 50). In what is 'more than a joke' and 'a refusal to be quite so serious about categories, and to let categories sit a bit lightly with the complexities of the world' (Franklin and Haraway 2017: 50), Haraway proclaims herself as a 'compost-ist' rather than a posthumanist (Haraway 2015a: 161). She argues that this rich matter of human–nonhuman entanglements can include non-living things (like digital technologies and digital data): 'I don't think compost excludes cyborgian politics. It doesn't exclude cyborg entities at all' (Franklin and Haraway 2017: 54). As Haraway points out, compost heaps often involve non-organic materials, such as plastics and metals. Her 'tentacular thinking' draws attention to the connections between things in this dense entanglement of objects (Haraway 2016), while her compost metaphor highlights the circular and generative relationship between life, death and decay (Franklin and Haraway 2017).

The tropes of companion species and compost may be taken up to think about the ways in which humans generate, materialize and engage with their lively digital data. Thrift (2014) has described the new 'hybrid beings' that are comprised of digital data and human flesh. Adopting Haraway's companion species trope allows for the extension of this idea by acknowledging the vitalities of digital data about humans and the relational nature of our interactions with these data. This way of thinking goes to the heart of how we might begin to theorize our data selves in the context of vitalities and agencies, highlighting the relationality and sociality that connect humans with technologies. We might also think about how personal data not only cohabit with us but are part of us, co-evolving and growing together. These human–data assemblages are combinations of nature/culture. The companion species and compost tropes suggest both the vitality of these assemblages and also the possibilities of developing a productive relationship, recognizing our mutual interdependencies, vulnerabilities and potentials.

Matterings and agential cuts

Karen Barad's agential realism perspective brings together discourse and materiality, acknowledging that 'matter and meaning are mutually articulated' (Barad 2007: 152). Barad draws attention to the importance of focusing analysis on how boundaries between phenomena are enacted, always involving choices about exclusions as well as inclusions. Barad (2003) further notes that humans do not know about the world because they are observing from outside it. Rather, they know the world because they are inseparably part of it. Epistemology and ontology cannot, therefore, be separated. 'Onto-epistem-ology – the study of practices of knowing and being – is probably a better way to think about the kind of understandings that are needed' (Barad 2003: 829). She contends that the practices of making these continuous and dynamic distinctions (including discursive practices which delimit what can be said) are part of agency: 'Agency is not an attribute but the ongoing reconfigurings of the world' (Barad 2003: 818).

Barad also emphasizes the distributed and performative nature of agency – it is not possessed by any one actor, human or nonhuman. Rather it is generated with and through relationships between humans and nonhumans: 'agency is an enactment, a matter of possibilities for reconfiguring entanglements' (Barad in Dolphijn and Van der Tuin 2012: 54). Barad's concept of 'intra-action' (as opposed to 'inter-action') signals the idea that entities are not individuated actors possessing their own agencies. Entities are configured and reconfigured through relational encounters of a diverse array of human and nonhuman actors. This includes the forces of agency, which are emergent in very specific sets of practices and must constantly be enacted and re-enacted (Barad 2003; 2007). Intra-action also involves what Barad (2014) calls 'agential cuts': ways in which differences are enacted. An agential cut identifies the boundaries of a phenomenon, grouping certain attributes together as part of this enactment as the same time as other attributes are excluded. Agential cuts make meaning from the potentially infinite sources that are available. As such, they are ways of making matter come to matter – indeed, of mattering. A specific intra-action enacts an agential cut, which works to make a distinction between phenomena. This cut can be viewed as a moment of making and learning. For this reason, Barad refers to agential cuts as 'cutting-together-apart' and 'entangling-differentiating' (Barad in Kleinman 2018: 80). This philosophy of agential realism views the making of differences and distinctions as part of intra-actions between agents and highlights their inherent instability (Barad in Kleinman 2018).

The concept of intra-action draws attention to how subjects and objects emerge via their engagements, as they respond to and enact each other. Barad highlights the importance of responsibility. Her definition of responsibility is more akin to responsiveness, or as Barad (in Kleinman 2018: 81) puts it, 'response-ability': the ability to respond. She goes on to note that the range of possible responses are conditioned and constrained by practices of engagement. For Barad, the queering of responsibility acknowledges the spaces and historicities of these practices. In a more-than-human approach, responsibility is not an obligation chosen by the human subject, but a relational intra-action of becoming and not-becoming. 'That is, responsibility is an iterative (re)opening up to, an enabling of responsiveness' (Barad in Kleinman 2018: 81). Barad's concept of 'responsibility', indeed, is 'not about the right response, but rather a matter of inviting, welcoming, and enabling the response of the Other' (Barad interviewed in Kleinman 2018: 81). She notes that responsibility is integral to intra-active becoming and unbecoming.

The effects of difference are a key focus of Barad's work. Barad (2007) critiques 'reflexive practice' as a mode of research, as this approach attempts to fix in time and place a specific understanding. Reflexive practice involves identifying a materialization of what is assumed to exist. In contrast, what Barad (2014) calls 'diffractive analysis' works to identify differences and alternative ways of being and doing, including how differences are made and what is excluded from decisions about what matters. From this perspective, what counts as 'truth' is always contingent, contextual and emergent, dependent on enactments of agential cuts. Analysis is directed at identifying these choices and the possibilities that they entail and close off. This may involve focusing attention on how humans and nonhumans differentiate themselves from other phenomena.

In their analysis of the vitality of media, Kember and Zylinska (2012) use the concept of the agential cut to argue that any attempt to impose meaning and order is an intervention (a cut) that produces specific effects, and is inevitably part of the matter it seeks to observe or document. They represent photography as a specific cut in meaning, a way of delimiting from all the choices available what can be recorded and displayed, and therefore, how meaning can be generated. It is the medium by which things are brought into being by humans and nonhumans (e.g., cameras) working together. Photography makes agential cuts that produce life forms rather than simply documenting them. 'It is a way of giving form to matter' (Kember and Zylinska 2012: 84).

Intra-actions with and enactments of personal data may be viewed as one such mode of differentiation. The digital devices and software used to generate data about humans work fundamentally to differentiate certain aspects of embodied practices and properties from others, using highly specific modes of measurement that tend to seek to quantify these practices and properties and render them more visible than other bodily attributes. Adopting this perspective, digitized information about people can also be viewed as a mediation of human activities and embodiments and as enacting agential cuts in defining these activities and embodiments. Personal data are one form of mediation of people's activities, preferences and habits, collected via their interactions online or using apps and wearable devices. Bodily capacities such as energy expenditure and intake, steps taken, pulse rate or weight, images taken using digital cameras and responses to other people's online engagements such as likes and shares: all become mediated through algorithmic processes and digital modes of storage. This mediation often involves quantification (how many steps taken, how many calories consumed or expended, how many likes or shares a post or status update receives) but may also involve devices such as facial recognition software and hashtags, which serve to identify and curate personal data, or geolocation software, which positions the details in the time and place they were generated. These initial processes of mediation are then open to almost infinite acts of remediation, as these data circulate and are repurposed in the digital data economy.

An agential cut, therefore, can be viewed as making and giving meaning to human–data assemblages. The industry of data mining and profiling is a compelling example of how different datasets on people can be harvested and recombined to generate profiles on people through processes of continually enacting agential cuts. So too, when people seek to make sense of their personal data, they are performing agential cuts.

Thing-power and enchantment

Affective forces are important elements of the agential capacities, vitalities and intensities generated by human–nonhuman assemblages. In her work, Barad considers how the affective force of matter contributes to its vital properties. She argues that:

> Matter itself is not a substrate or medium for the flow of desire. Materiality itself is always already a desiring dynamism, a reiterative reconfiguring, energized and energizing, enlivened and enlivening. I have been particularly interested in how matter comes to matter. How matter makes itself felt ... Matter feels, converses, suffers, desires, yearns and remembers. (Barad in Dolphijn and Van der Tuin 2012: 59)

In her books *The Enchantment of Modern Life* (2001) and *Vibrant Matter* (2009), Jane Bennett also draws attention to the capacity of human–nonhuman assemblages to generate affective forces and vitalities. Bennett (2009: 112, original emphasis) argues that a vital materialism approach 'better captures an "alien" quality of our own flesh, and in so doing reminds humans of the very *radical* character of the (fractious) kinship between the human and the nonhuman'. Bennett's concept of 'thing-power', or 'the curious ability of inanimate things to animate, to act, to product effects dramatic and subtle' (2004: 351), emphasizes the vibrant agential capacities of human–nonhuman assemblages. Thing-power is a dynamic flow of energy between and with the components of assemblages. Bennett emphasizes the sensory dimensions that are part of understanding and feeling the force of vital materiality. She describes thing-power as 'the strange ability of ordinary, man-made items to exceed their status as objects and to manifest traces of independence or aliveness, constituting the outside of our own experiences' (2009: xvi).

For Bennett, it is thing-power, and the affects and vitalities that contribute to this force, that give material objects agency as they come together with humans. She argues that the concept of thing-power emphasizes the intimacy of humans and nonhumans: the ways in which they are so closely intertwined in the moments when 'human being and thinghood overlap' (2004: 349). She further elaborates that thing-power is not located in one specific object alone, but rather is a function of the grouping of different things in an assemblage, each operating in conjunction with the others (including humans) (Bennett 2004: 354). Thing-power includes the ability to create effects and affects that can be enabling or disabling. Bennett refers to the 'material recalcitrance' (2004: 348) of cultural forms in emphasizing that these human–nonhuman assemblages may pose resistances to human intentions.

Bennett uses the concept of enchantment in her work on vital materialities to encapsulate these capacities and intensities. *The Enchantment of Modern Life* (2001) is an attempt to understand how mundane activities and objects acquire and inspire strong affects that animate investments and attachments. Bennett (2001: 3) discusses these affects as contributing to the enchanting features of aspects of modern life, or what she describes as 'the wonder of minor experiences'. She contends that: 'To be enchanted is to be struck and shaken by the extraordinary that lives amid the familiar and the everyday' (Bennett 2001: 4). Bennett defines enchantment as a mood that may include fear and liveliness as well as wonder and excitement, often involving a surprise encounter in which the unexpected happens. She views enchantment as a counter to the disenchantment that often pervades late modernity, in which the world is considered as ruined and meaningless. She argues that enchantment can be encountered spontaneously, but it can also be deliberately developed, or cultivated.

Importantly for my analysis in this book, although Bennett's major focus is on humans' ethical engagements with the ecosystem, she recognizes technologies and mass-produced commodities as possible sites of enchantment, particularly in her analysis of the agency of material objects. One example she provides is that of the electrical power grid assemblage (Bennett 2005). Bennett shows that the discrete elements of this human–nonhuman assemblage work together as a flowing system that largely functions well, despite regular events and energies that threaten it (e.g., damage from animals, trees or wind, human mistakes, interference from electromagnetic fields). In this discussion, Bennett again refers to enchantment, using the term 'enchanted materialism' to describe a kind of vitalism possessed by human–nonhuman assemblages (Bennett 2005: 446). This vitalism, she argues, is 'alive with movement and with a certain power of expression' (Bennett 2005: 446).

The concept of enchanted materialism emphasizes the heterogeneous, mobile and emergent nature of thing-power, elements which contribute to its vitality and volatility. Bennett (2004: 349) discusses the importance of fostering a 'receptivity to thing-power' and a consonant awareness of its impact on ecology and implications for environmental sustainability. While she does not make direct reference to digital data about human bodies, this is clearly a prime potential object of attention for future work on this topic.

In a completely different literature, the concept of enchantment is sometimes employed in the world of tech development to explain why users become interested in digital objects, adopt them, and continue to use them. Claims to 'magical' novel digital technologies are rife in industry promotions that attempt to demonstrate how artificial intelligence, 'smart' objects and personal data will change users' lives for the better (Elish and boyd 2018). Attempting to create affordances that will generate the enchanting qualities of digital technologies has become a key element of design cultures.

In the opening pages of his book *Enchanted Objects*, for example, David Rose (2014) addresses digital technology designers working on 'smart' objects. He discusses the 'personality' of digital objects and how designers should bear in mind what type of personality their object should possess: 'Domineering or polite? Should our technologies look cold or cute? Do we want to interact with them as smart tools or caring agents?' (Rose 2014: xii). For Rose, as a digital technology designer, enchantment should be a central feature of these technologies so that users are attracted to take them up and find pleasure in their use, and in doing so, create the emotional connections to which he refers in his book's opening lines. Rose goes on to explain how important digital devices (hardware) are in generating these connections, in concert with software that serves to animate the devices. Both software and hardware should ideally work together as an interface that can conjure up enchantment. The sensory dimensions of smart devices' materiality are integral, he argues, to enchantment: not only how they look, but also how they feel when touched, and how they work with embodied senses, expanding and enhancing sensory capacities.

Others working in technological design have also commented on the growing tendency of humans to invest digital devices with animistic or magical properties. It is argued that the developing Internet of Things, where digital objects communicate with each other, as well as the increasing array of digital devices that can be worn on and with human bodies, contribute to these enchantments because they are so seamlessly integrated into people's embodied mundane routines. For Betti Marenko (2014), the objects that Rose views as enchanted can best be understood using a neo-animist paradigm. She contends that the more digital devices become domesticated and pervasive, the more we tend to think of them in pre-modern ways as possessing life-forces or magical properties. These 'smart' objects are increasingly both animate and inanimate in the ways we think of and respond to them. Marenko claims that we need a neo-animist paradigm to understand our relationships with these objects, including our multisensory engagements with devices: the ways we touch, talk to and hear as well as see them. The enchantment of digital objects reaches its apotheosis when they are so well integrated into our lives that we hardly view them as separate from our bodies/selves, and the more we experience them as 'smart' or intuitive.

With van Allen, Marenko has gone on to examine the ways in which what they call 'animistic design' can be used to reimagine digitized human–nonhuman encounters (Marenko and van Allen 2016). They define animistic design as a form of speculative design, which 'is capable of fostering affects, sensibilities and thoughts that capitalize on the uncertain, the unpredictable and the nonlinear, and their capacity to trigger creative pathways' (Marenko and van Allen 2016: 52).

In bringing Bennett's concepts of vitality, enchantment and thing-power with this approach to the design and user experience of digital objects and digital data, the ways in which sociomaterial phenomena such as digital data assemblages can participate in acts of enchantment (and disenchantment) can be explored. These perspectives and concepts emphasize the affective forces that can be generated with and through digital media and data. They portray digital technological assemblages as possessing power, intensities and agencies as they come together with humans.

Composing, decomposing and recomposing data

Anthropologists have also called attention to the lively agencies of the entanglements of humans and matter. The ethnographic and historical scholarship of Tim Ingold and his collaborator Elizabeth Hallam, both anthropologists who write about material cultures, contribute to concepts of perceiving and learning as part of embodied practices with lively objects. Ingold and Hallam have written about processes of making and living with things, emphasizing the role of creativity, improvisation and learning by doing. Ingold's book *Being Alive* (2011), as the title suggests, focuses attention on the vitalities of everyday life. He draws attention to the ways in which nonhuman elements of the world beyond written texts inspire and challenge human thinking, learning and experience. Ingold conceptualizes the notion of life being lived along lines and uses the term 'meshwork' to encapsulate his interest in the 'interwoven threads' in which lines come together or cross over each other, in creating mesh rather than a network (2011: xii). Ingold argues that human living involves observation, or being alive to the world. He notes that growing and changing are parts of any form of life. Humans perceive and learn about the world as they move through it, and simultaneously act to generate or transform it.

In his book *Making* (2013), Ingold focuses his ethnographic analyses on the practices involved in making objects, and how learning is part of these processes. Using the organic metaphor of growing, Ingold connects embodiment and learning. He argues that:

> the only way one can really know things – that is, from the very inside of one's being – is through a process of self-discovery. To know things you have to grow into them, and let them grow in you, so that they become a part of who you are. (Ingold 2013: 1)

Ingold further contends that there should be more focus on anthropological research on the movements of materials, following their paths as they mix or interact with each other and materialize into objects, and then decompose: 'We discover, then, that materials are active' (2011: 16). For Ingold (2013), material artefacts are never fixed or completed. Because they are open to new meanings and uses, they are always in a process of becoming something else. As they move into new or different contexts, artefacts change in meaning, even if not always in shape. Ingold and Hallam (2014) discuss the emergent properties of artefacts, emphasizing the new ways in which artefacts can be used and reused and change during the process. Just as making and learning are never finished, artefacts 'pass from one form of life to another' (Ingold and Hallam 2014: 2). Ingold and Hallam emphasize that growing things need not be only living things, using the examples of mineral deposits and crystals. Growth, indeed, is 'the fundamental condition of beings and things in a world that is always surpassing itself' (Ingold and Hallam 2014: 3). They point out that an inevitable part of growth is decomposition and decay. Out of this rotting of matter springs new matter, continuing the growth cycle.

In her empirical scholarship, Hallam has focused predominantly on how dead bodies or other human remains (such as bones) have been portrayed and used in the context of museum anatomical displays, as artefacts for learning. She examines their contributions to fields of knowledge, and how these displays are creatively made. As she notes, anatomical displays of human bodies 'cut across the categories of the organic and artefactual' (Hallam 2016: 8). Hallam (2010; 2016) uses the term 'articulation' to describe the ways in which various actors seek to make sense of parts of human bodies they are working with. For example, articulation refers both to how bones from a specific skeleton can be fitted together and how bones can be used and inserted into a range of diverse narratives and social relations, depending on the context. Bones, she argues, are relational entities. They have different meanings based on the historical, political and physical settings in which they are located, and the intentions of the human actors working to make sense of them: archaeologists, biologists, artists, historians, relatives or many other potential actors.

As Hallam (2010) points out, it is far from the case that bones, once interred, are inert and no longer meaningful. They can be disinterred and used for many other purposes. Bones have been used in a multitude of ways as decorative, artistic or religious artefacts. While commonly thought of as 'dead', therefore, human bones are very much alive, in terms of their changing meanings and uses and the capacity they possess to arouse affect and action. They can be moved into very different contexts and take on different agential capacities. Thus, for example, human bones can be exhumed, reburied, turned into powder, brought into an art or museum exhibition, each time developing new meanings. The material properties of human bones facilitate many forms of display for mourning, commemorative, political, religious, symbolic, historical, heritage, decorative and artistic purposes.

Recent scholarship in information and archival studies has begun to acknowledge the multisensory dimensions of humans' enactments of information and archival material. The 'archival body' is a term used by Jamie Lee (2016) to describe the embodied experience of handling archival artefacts about people's lives, and also to encapsulate the assemblage that is the conglomeration of a person's life and body as it is represented through archival materials. As she notes, these records of human lives can have intense emotional resonances for the researchers who are viewing, smelling and touching them. The archival bodies of the researcher and the researched are always in motion, making meaning together.

Other writers on the affective resonances of archival material have called attention to the stories of persecution, violence, discrimination, racism and other aggressions that may be encountered by humans engaging with these materials. As they point out, archivists can be witnesses to occurrences and experiences of social injustices and criminal activities: events that can generate intense affective and sensory forces (Cifor 2016; Cifor and Gilliland 2016). Thus, for example, writing from the perspective of an information studies researcher sifting through historical archives, Marika Cifor (2017) employed feminist new materialism to identify the liveliness of analogue archival material about lesbian, bisexual, queer, gay, transgender and intersex (LBQGTI) communities. As she observes, these materials include not only paper documents, but also parts of human bodies: for example, the hair of assassinated gay activist Harvey Milk encased in an envelope, and his blood traces on his garments that have also been preserved in the archives. She finds other bodily traces and fluids on documents, or what she calls 'the detritus matter of queer bodies in archives' (Cifor 2017: 6). Cifor's bodily experiences in handling and viewing these materials, as she notes, highlight the intimacy of archival collecting and research and the sensory and affective forces that are generated in these gatherings. In these ways, these archival materials, which are both of the (dead) human body and engaged with by (currently living) human bodies, mediated through the infrastructures of historical archiving, are imbued with vitalities and vibrancies. These dead human materials are reanimated with affective force and meaning through the archivist's enactments. For example, Cifor found that touching Milk's bloodstained garments was for her an intense and intimate affective and sensory experience. 'The materiality of the blood in the archives transforms him from icon to man, creating a new relation between us' (Cifor 2017: 12).

While decomposition can lead to loss of information, it can also allow more-than-human actors to participate in narrative communication. Caitlin DeSilvey (2006), for example, provides an account of working as researcher on an abandoned homestead in the US state of Montana. She describes the 'deposits of ambiguous matter' (DeSilvey 2006: 319) that she dealt with in excavating the homestead's ruins and trying to make sense of what objects were there and how they were used. These objects were both visibly very decomposed and vital with living creatures such as moulds, maggots and mice. As DeSilvey points out, such degraded objects threaten order, arousing disgust because of their blurring of the boundaries between clean and proper (and indeed, valuable) matter, and waste or dirt. Value judgements must be brought into play in deciding what matter should matter and which should be discarded or ignored, and left to further rot. In these contexts, humans and nonhumans work together to create, recreate, use and degrade artefacts. The living and the non-living come together to create new forms of life: as in the paper magazines that become slowly eaten away by insects or rodents.

DeSilvey (2006: 323) describes how difficult it can be for anthropologists and cultural geographers to decide what is an 'artefact' (defined as an object that is human-made) and an 'ecofact' (an object made from other-than-human engage-ments with elements such as climate and biology). Often, they are both. Curation involves fixing objects in a certain state, so that decay is slowed or halted and the item is preserved to act as a bearer of cultural memory. In these ways, artefacts can create new forms of life – be revitalized – as they enter new contexts of meaning, value and use. These strategies of preservation, however, destroy some cultural traces of the object at the same time as other elements are protected.

Archaeologists are also centrally concerned with handling and preserving material artefacts, and feminist materialist theory, as well as Ingold's work, has begun to make an impact in this discipline. The ever-changing relational and entangled nature of historical artefacts has received attention. This approach puts understanding assemblages of things and humans at the centre of archaeology, acknowledging that the meanings and purposes of objects are not reducible to their components. From new materialist archaeology comes the insight that the affordances of things change in time and space and may be limiting to human agency in some contexts and enabling in others. It is focused on the things themselves and how they are dependent on and connected with other things rather than solely what purpose they serve for humans. Relational ontologies, therefore, are important to this approach in archaeology, with a particular interest in the notion that matter contains 'unactualized potential' (Jones and Alberti 2016: 26) rather than specific inherent properties, and that this potential is only actualized via relations with humans and other things.

From these perspectives on material cultures, although human bodies may be culturally defined as dead – and in the case of bodies that are archaeological artefacts, dead for hundreds or thousands of years – death is more of a continuum and the body's materialities are changeable and transmutable. Elements of a human body that is defined as an archaeological artefact have responded to the physical environment over a long time, taking on some of the environmental elements and giving back materials to the environment. This body possesses vitality and agential capacities, potentially animating futures. While it is buried, the archaeological body gradually disperses itself into the environment as it decomposes, releasing and recirculating its energies by recomposing the matter it becomes. When it is excavated by archaeologists and analysed, its composition becomes reconfigured via scientific analyses (identifying DNA, bone minerality composition, isotopes and so on) and it begins to influence narratives of the present by contributing to archaeological knowledges (Fredengren 2018).

These perspectives offer important insights into understanding the onto-ethico-epistemologies of data selves. They go well beyond the idea that information generates knowledge or self-understanding. Instead, this scholarship focuses on lived practices and how they develop and change over time. Learning is therefore viewed as a continuing process rather than a fixed-term event, and one which involves acts of making, improvisation and adjusting to change. It is also a profoundly embodied experience, not just located in cognition.

Hallam's concept of articulation draws attention to the work involved in bringing human remains together, the multifarious ways in which this may be achieved and the consequent vitality of the meanings and capacities these remains can take on. Her discussions of the lively capacities of human bones also have much to offer an onto-ethico-epistemology of digital data about humans. Like human bones, human digital data only make sense in the contexts in which they are located. Like human bones, they have infinite capacities for taking on new meaning. Like bones, our personal digital data are reliquaries of our humanity, testaments to our lived experiences and unique identity. These data are materializations of selfhood that both represent elements of the self and also require attentive labour to generate value for those who make them. They possess biovalue, just as body parts, cells and tissues do. Personal data, in other words, can be viewed as a new type of human remains, one that is potentially open to a multitude of repurposing and reconfiguring, leading to many kinds of value for a diverse range of actors. Like human remains, personal data may also lose their potency and vibrancy, their agential capacities to affect and be affected.

The processes of creating the meanings of cultural artefacts may be interrupted, broken, disrupted or lost. But this state of decay or deadness may not be permanent. So too, personal digital data may not be useful initially, but can become meaningful later. Like bones and other artefacts, they can be articulated with other data and take on more value. In the global digital data economy, the economic or research value of joining up disparate datasets about individuals to create detailed profiles of them has intensified. If we adopt

Haraway's compost metaphor, even when digital data (or bones) have decayed, they may still possess potential vital capacities to grow new assemblages. Digital data can be 'cleaned' and made more useful or valuable, or they can be recomposed with other datasets, again generating new meaning. They may also reach a point where decomposition is so advanced that repair or recomposition cannot take place.

Here again, vitalities and agential capacities can be considered key to the ways in which humans respond to the elements of the environments with which they form assemblages. According to Frost (2016: 153), the 'cultural' dimension of what she calls 'biocultural creatures' is representational, political and social but also biological, temporal and spatial. Together these dimensions work to compose and de/recompose humans, providing the conditions in which they live, move and grow (or are 'cultured', as Frost puts it). Humans, in turn, make and remake their habits through their continued presence in them and through intentional and unintentional adjustments they make to them. De/recomposition takes place in different ways and timescales for humans, from the micro level of the cells to the macro level of movement of the body through space. There are constraints on how humans respond to their environments that delimit what they can and cannot do and in what transformations they participate (Frost 2016).

If this approach is applied to digital data practices and their configurations, then focusing attention on the language that is employed to describe digital data, viewing digital data as objects that have both discursive and material effects and that are constantly changing, recognizing the processes of tinkering (experimenting, adapting) that occur in relation to digital data and the spaces in which these processes take place are all important to developing an understanding of the ontology of digital data and our relationship with them. Data about humans can and do 'live on' after the humans from whose flesh they were generated have expired and decomposed. These data can potentially have lives that extend well into the foreseeable future. Other forms of documentation of human life have existed for millennia (going back to rock paintings and other material forms of documentation).

Digital data can be preserved in digital archives and can take on new forms of life well after the humans who have created them have died. This continued liveliness of personal data, indeed, has created some dilemmas about how to define ownership and stewardship of the 'digital assets' of dead people and what should happen to their social media profiles and content (Bollmer 2013; Öhman and Floridi 2018).

Summary

There are several related themes that emerge in the scholarship I have reviewed in this chapter. All adopt a more-than-human approach that: recognizes that humans and nonhumans are entangled in hybrid, unstable and generative ways; takes into account the importance of considering the distributed agency and vital capacities ('thing-power') of human–nonhuman assemblages; places an emphasis on the embodied, sensory and otherwise material nature of meaning, knowing, perceiving and making as part of human embodiment; directs attention to the changing meanings of artefacts as they move into different assemblages and the work required to articulate these assemblages; and highlights the importance of identifying and tracing the ways in which humans and nonhumans are intermeshed, the enactments and practices that are involved, and the effects of these on human lives.

These approaches use organic and animist metaphors and concepts to think through the nature of human–nonhuman assemblages. These metaphors and concepts draw attention to the vibrant, hybrid and emergent nature of these assemblages. They can contribute to new ways of conceptualizing human–data assemblages and how people incorporate data into their bodies and lives. These proliferating data–human assemblages, as they are ceaselessly configured and reconfigured, emerge beyond our bodies/selves and into the wild of digital data economies and circulations. They are purposed and repurposed by second and third parties and even more actors beyond our reckoning as they are assembled and reassembled, becoming complex digital 'compost'. Even as our data selves engage in their own lives, they are still part of us and we remain part of them. We may interact with them or not; we may be allowed access to them or not; we may be totally unaware of them or we may engage in purposeful collection and use of them.

In developing close studies of quotidian experiences of making, doing and living with personal data, an analysis founded on perspectives from the work of the scholars I have here discussed serves to highlight the intertwined, embodied, affective and multisensory nature of known, knower and knowing. Such an analysis can involve both a reflexive analysis, focusing on the shared tacit norms, assumptions and discourses that underpin practices, and a diffractive analysis that directs attention to what is different or resistant, and identifying new or alternative possibilities. Both approaches can work towards a better understanding of how and in what contexts personal data can assume importance and significance in people's lives; and in others, lose their vitality, value and potential for opening up productive agencies. These issues are taken up and explored in more detail in the chapters that follow.

3

Materializing Data

In this chapter, I examine the ways in which personal data are 'materialized': how they are represented in words and images or rendered into tangible things that can be responded to in multisensory ways. These materializations have profound implications for how we make, think and feel about our data, how we make sense of our data and how human–data assemblages intra-act and are made to matter.

Digital data metaphors and imagery

We have to work hard to find figures of speech and ways of thinking to encapsulate the ontology of digital data. The term 'data' is closely associated with 'information'. Information as a term is subject to a wide range of (often debated) definitions in the academic literature. It usually involves the assumption that there are structures, correlations and patterns involved in the organization and communication of meaning. Information tends to be imbued with the pragmatic meanings of rational thought processes and material that can contribute to acquiring and using knowledge. It has use and value based on these attributes (Buckland 1991). Digital data, as forms of information that have been collected and processed using digital technologies, are often portrayed as more accurate and insightful than many other information sources (Kitchin 2014; Lupton 2015a), particularly if they are presented in metric formats (Beer 2016).

The concept of digital data, at first glance, appears to describe a wholly immaterial phenomenon that does not engage the senses: there seems to be nothing to look at, touch, hear, smell or taste. The metaphors and other figures of language employed to describe digital data are attempts to conceptualize and make sense of these novel forms of information and their ontologies. Even as digital technologies continue to generate and process detailed and often very intimate and revealing information about people's bodies, social relationships, emotions, practices and preferences, prevailing discourses on these data frequently work to depersonalize and dehumanize them. The use of the term 'data' to describe these details signals a way of viewing and treating them, presenting these details as raw materials, ripe for processing and exploitation to make them give up their meaning (Gitelman and Jackson 2013; Räsänen and Nyce 2013). Once they have become defined and labelled as 'data', these details about people's lives tend to be imagined as impersonal, scientific and neutral. They have been extracted from their embodied, sensory and affective contexts, rendered into digitized formats and viewed as material for life optimization, self-knowledge, research, managerial, security or commercial purposes.

Many references to 'big data' – or very large databases generated from online interactions and digital sensor technologies – represent them as anonymized massive collections of details that are valuable commodities, open to profitable exploitation. The World Economic Forum's report (2011) describing big data as 'the new oil', 'a valuable resource of the 21st century' and a 'new asset class' is an influential example of this metaphor. Metaphors of fluidities also tend to be employed when describing digital data. Digital data are popularly imagined to stream, flow and circulate in the ephemeral digital data economy, emitting imperceptibly from digital devices, flying through the air to lodge in and move between computing clouds as if made up of vaporized water. Many metaphors of digital data use words and phrases that denote overwhelming power and mobilities, again often referring to large bodies of uncontrollable water; the data 'deluge', 'flood', 'ocean' and even 'tsunami' that constantly appear in popular accounts of big data in particular. These figures of speech are used to denote feelings of being overwhelmed by large, powerful masses of data that appear to be difficult to control or make sense of in their volume (Lupton 2015a). Still other metaphors represent data as 'exhaust', 'trails' or 'breadcrumbs', denoting the by-products of other interactions on digital networks. These metaphors suggest a tangible, perceivable form of digital data, albeit tiny, that require effort to discern and give up their value.

In her essay on digital data, Melissa Gregg (2015a) employs a number of other metaphors she devised to encapsulate the meanings of data. Data 'agents' suggests the capacities of data to work with algorithms to generate connections: matches, suggestions and relationships between social phenomena that otherwise would not be created. Gregg gives the examples of recommendation sites and online dating services, which connect strangers and their experiences with each other in ways that were previously unimaginable. She goes on to suggest that 'In these instances, data acts rather more like our appendage, our publicist, even our shadow' (Gregg 2015a: 60). Gregg also employs the metaphor of data 'sweat' (another liquid metaphor) in the attempt to emphasize the embodied nature of data, emerging or leaking from within the body to the outside in an uncontrolled manner to convey information about that body, including how hard it is working or how productive it is. Data 'sweat', therefore, can be viewed as a materialization of labour. She then suggests the concept of data 'trash' (similar to the 'exhaust' metaphor). Data 'trash' is data that are in some way useless or potentially polluting or hazardous: Gregg links this metaphor with the environmental effects generated by creating, storing and processing data in data centres (see also Hogan 2018). Both the metaphors of data 'sweat' and 'trash' suggest the materiality of digitized information as well as its ambivalent and dynamic status as it moves between ascriptions of high value and useless – or even disgusting – waste product.

Visual images are also frequently employed in popular culture in the attempt to give meaning to digital data. An analysis of images used to represent big data in online editions of the *New York Times* and the *Washington Post* (Pentzold et al. 2019) found that they tended to fall into several categories: using large-scale numbers, interpretive abstract renditions, showing numbers or graphs on smartphone or computer screens, images of data warehouses and devices that generate data, robots, datafied individuals, and meteorological imagery such as clouds. A dominant visual image involved photographic images of people working in the big data industry, such as data scientists, 'nerds' and 'geeks' (overwhelmingly male) and logos of internet companies. The researchers compared these images with those found on a general Google image search for 'big data' and also on Wikipedia and the image platforms Fotolia, Flickr and Pinterest. They noted that the images they found on these platforms were very homogeneous, featuring the colour blue, the words 'big data' written large, binary numbers, network structures and surveillant human eyes.

Not all digital datasets are about humans. They may relate to nonhuman animals or other living things (e.g., in agricultural or ecological data), or to climate variables, goods and services or a multitude of other aspects of the world that can be recorded using digital technologies. However, as I outlined in chapter 1, many big datasets do record details about people and their lives. These kinds of descriptions suggest that big datasets (including those drawn from people's lives and experiences) are natural resources that are unproblematically open to exploration, mining and processing for profit. The personal details about people contained within these massive datasets are represented as commodities for exploitation by others. It is telling that the human elements of these images largely include men working in data analytics rather than the range of people who generate data or who may make use of their own data as part of their everyday lives.

In these sociotechnical imaginaries, the status of personal data as human, or at least partly human, entities is submerged in the excitement about how best to exploit these details as material commodities. Their liveliness is represented in ways that suggest their economic potential as nonhuman organic materials (streams, flows, oil, clouds, breadcrumbs). Yet conversely, another dominant discourse about personal data, which is particularly promulgated by the data profiling industry and civil society privacy advocates, is that these details are all-too-human or even excessively human: intensely intimate and revealing of people's uniquely human character-istics. When I performed my own Google image search using the term 'personal data', the images that were returned by the search again featured the colour blue, male figures and binary numbers. Notably, several images showed a pen and a paper form with the words 'personal information' at the top, perhaps in an attempt to respond to the apparent immate-riality of digitized information by rendering it in analogue forms with which many people would be familiar. Images using locks and keys as metaphors were also dominant, suggesting the value of personal data but also how closed they are to people who may want to make use of them. When I used the search term 'personal data privacy', new images were introduced in addition to those appearing under 'personal data'. These included images of spy-like or Big Brother surveillance figures and also images showing human hands protectively attempting to cover computer keyboards or screens, as if to elude the gaze of these spying figures as people used their devices.

Some metaphors and imagery attempt to humanize digital data profiles about people. The term 'digital footprint' is frequently used as a way of suggesting that the digital traces left as people interact with online technologies and 'smart' technologies are a form of biometric identification. Images of digital footprints often feature a collection of logos or the names of internet companies, zeros and ones or images of computer networks gathered into the shape of a human footprint. In another example, a series of 2018 British adver-tisements for the BBH London & Experian data analytics company used the 'data self' concept in an attempt to emphasize the similarities of these profiles to the people from whom they are generated. Six versions of this ad featured photographs of comedian Marcus Brigstocke and his 'data self', a person who looked exactly like him. As one of the ads, headlined 'Meet Your Data Self' claimed: 'Your Data Self is the version of you that companies see when you apply for things like credit cards, loans and mortgages. You two should get acquainted'. One of the ads, headlined, 'What shape is your Data Self in?', showed the comedian looking at his doppelgänger lifting a heavy barbell. The copy read, 'If your Data Self looks good to lenders, you're more likely to be approved for credit. That's a weight off. Get to know your Data Self at Experian.co.uk.' Another ad asked, 'Is your Data Self making the right impression?', depicting the comedian, dressed in casual clothes, shaking hands with his more formally dressed (in suit and tie) data self. It is notable that here again, the human and his 'data self' portrayed in every iteration of this campaign is a white, youngish male. Seemingly no thought was given by the company and its advertising agency to depicting a more diverse range of people and their data selves.

As I noted in chapters 1 and 2, many new artificial intelligence technologies are promoted in media accounts and industry marketing materials as magical or enchanted, suggesting functionality, benevolence, problem-solving and other benefits for users beyond the level of human expectation, understanding or perception, and with no cost or harm to humans. These portrayals typically present a future that is tantalizingly just out of reach rather than fully realized (Elish and boyd 2018). The Internet of Things is now sometimes described as the 'Internet of Me': a more-than-human assemblage of objects and data ceaselessly monitoring people in the interests of improving their lives through better knowledge about themselves. Proponents of the Internet of Me make claims such as those by entrepreneur Matt Anderson: 'imagine tech working in your body at the biological level. Your body could express itself on its own, without you having to be in charge, to deliver more happiness, better health, whatever you truly need and want' (Anderson quoted in Wired Insider 2018). These sociotechnical imaginaries position devices and data as working together with human bodies in ways that devolve agency to the device. 'You' no longer have to be 'in charge' – instead, the device takes over.

Other imaginaries concerning the Internet of Me configure the idea of personal cloud computing, in which all people's personal data go to a centralized cloud computing repository where they will be able to access all their data (Carroll 2018). One online article on the Internet of Me features an image in which a human body is made from many different social media and other internet platform icons as well as coloured dots representing other data sources. Instead of an assemblage of flesh–bone–blood, the body is completely datafied and networked. Interestingly, this body is represented as an autonomous agent. The networks that generate data and keep the body vibrant and functioning are internal, not externalized to networks outside this socially alienated body. Data flows are contained within elements of the body rather than leaking outside it to other bodies. This suggests an imaginary in which the Internet of Me is neatly contained within the envelope of the body/self and thus able to control ingress and egress. This is an orderly closed system, one that confounds both utopian and dystopian imaginaries concerning the possibilities and risks of one's body/self being situated as just one node in vast and complex networked digital systems.

Due to the often sensitive and intimate nature of personal data, the many and varied uses to which they can be put to work and their potential to be of value to a wide range of actors and agencies beyond the individual, a set of dystopian imaginaries have begun to receive attention in public forums. The imaginaries often pivot on the belief that internet corporations have penetrating insights into the psyches and secrets of internet users.

Thus, for example, in his popular book *Everybody Lies: What the Internet Can Tell Us About Who We Really Are* (2017), self-proclaimed 'internet data expert' Seth Stephens-Davidowitz recounts his analysis of Google searches for certain topics or questions, using Google Trends (which shows relative frequency for searches) and Google AdWords (how frequently each search is made) as his tools. As his book's title suggests, Stephens-Davidowitz claims that this kind of analysis is a way of uncovering certain truths about people that they otherwise might not reveal to anyone: including their sexual proclivities, their racist tendencies and their sexist attitudes. He contends that the types of questions and words people use in Google Search reveal these attitudes and secret desires or feelings: or 'who we really are'. In the opening pages of his book, Stephens-Davidowitz argues that this kind of analysis can answer such pressing social questions as how many men have sex with men, whether advertising works and who cheats on their taxes. Stephens-Davidowitz's book has provided the basis for many commentaries in the popular media about similar issues: how well the internet can document people's secret thoughts and desires and how data analysts can use these data to provide insights into social behaviours. Some academic researchers have also begun to imagine near-future scenarios such as 'Total Data', in which 'every human action, reaction, interaction, transaction, thought or desire is quantified, reified, recorded and used', as Peter Carew (2018: 357) writing in the *AI & Society* journal put it.

In the wake of various highly publicized data scandals, references to the use of personal data have begun to draw on military metaphors that suggest that data scientists, harvesters and profilers are the enemy of ordinary citizens. One example is an article that internet scholar Ian Bogost (2018) wrote for the *Atlantic*, in which he made hyperbolic claims about the agency of personal data. According to Bogost, 'the personal-data privacy war is long over, and you lost', because '[e]verything you have done has been recorded, munged, and spat back at you to benefit sellers, advertisers, and the brokers who service them'. As a result, Bogost claimed, 'The age of privacy nihilism is here, and it's time to face the dark hollow of its pervasive void'. He went on to argue: 'Now a batch of computer dorks know everything you say, do, dream or desire – even the stuff you're too ashamed to admit to yourself'. Bogost's statements, which were partly a response to the Cambridge Analytica/Facebook scandal, call on the language of warfare and repressive surveillance by commercial companies.

Adopting a similar tone in his keynote address in October 2018, Apple CEO Tim Cook (quoted in Salinas and Meredith 2018) claimed that these industries were 'weaponizing' 'our own information, from the everyday to the deeply personal' 'against us with military efficiency', and referred to the 'data industrial complex'. Cook argued that data profiling means that 'these scraps of data, each one harmless enough on its own, are carefully assembled, synthesized, traded, and sold'. As a result, he claimed, data companies 'know you better than you may know yourself. Your profile is then run through algorithms that can serve up increasingly extreme content, pounding our harmless preferences into hardened convictions'. This is the language of violence, suggesting that personal information, otherwise 'harmless', can be turned into a 'weapon' of assault. Cook's words suggest that knowledge about an individual, if placed in the wrong hands, becomes capable of harming them by turning 'preferences' into 'convictions'. He went on to claim that Apple had a very different perspective on personal data compared with these (unnamed) companies: 'treating [users'] personal data like the precious cargo it is'.

Creepy data

The year 2018 marked the 200-year anniversary of the publication of Mary Shelley's classic Gothic novel *Frankenstein, or the Modern Prometheus*. This novel has become a cultural icon, largely due to the figure of the creature, the strange monster cobbled together from parts of corpses by the scientist Dr Victor Frankenstein. Dr Frankenstein is obsessed with creating life from non-living matter. He eventually creates a creature which resembles a human in many aspects, although it is much larger and has an unearthly appearance that marks it as clearly not human. Frankenstein is repulsed by the creature, which escapes from his laboratory. The creature, for its part, finds its own appearance hideous, and experiences rejection from the people it encounters because it looks so strange and frightening. Eventually the creature turns murderous, wanting to wreak vengeance on its creator for its lonely and disturbed existence.

The story of Frankenstein's creature and its creator is a moral tale, vividly speculating on the ways in which humans' ambitions to tinker with nature can go badly wrong. A central theme in this tale is the figure of the creature itself, in its eerie, almost-human-like appearance and sensibility. The creature has human feelings and emotions, needs and desires, but it looks too strange and monstrous to be able to be accepted by humans, and its rage eventually overwhelms it. The novel raises important onto-ethico-epistemological questions about what it means to be human, how novel technologies can disturb the definition and meaning of the human, and how scientific innovation can threaten humanity. It demonstrates the power of affective responses when parts of humans come together in new ways to create new forms of human (or almost-human, or more-than-human) life.

These days, a range of speculative fiction accounts represent digital technologies and the personal data they generate as creating monstrous new formations of humanity. Thus, for example, many episodes of the dystopian speculative fiction series *Black Mirror* feature references to people's digitally monitored and archived data. In the most obvious reference to Frankenstein's monster, in the episode 'Be right back' (season 2), a grieving woman uses a digital service that draws on the archive of her dead husband's online interactions to first talk to a digitized version of him on the phone, then create him in the flesh. Although at first, she finds it comforting to have this post-death replicant of her partner with her, she soon finds it disturbing and annoying, as the replicant is not able to properly display the human quirks of the real man she knew and loved. It is human-like, but not human enough. In 'Nosedive' (season 3), people use their smart devices constantly to rank and rate each other, with the resultant data affecting their life opportunities. The episode 'Playtest' (season 3) depicts a computer game-like scenario, when people's memories are accessed by a digital device to make the game as frightening as possible by accessing their deepest fears. 'The entire history of you' (season 1) plot involves a man forcing his partner to 'rewind' her memories to prove her infidelity and, in so doing, destroys their relationship. In 'Arkangel' (season 4), a child is relentlessly monitored by her anxious mother using a digital device that reveals the girl's perspective on the world and monitors biometrics such as her heart rate and adrenaline levels. Once the girl reaches adolescence and becomes aware of the privacy invasion that she is subjected to, she is driven to anger and violence against her mother because of the violation she feels.

'Black Museum', the season 4 finale, was one of the darkest episodes of the series in its recounting of how a man's data profile encapsulating his consciousness and physical appearance is used to punish him and his family for the gratification of others. The episode tells the tale of a young woman who visits an unusual museum (the eponymous Black Museum) located in a remote desert location. The only visitor at the time, she is shown around by the museum's proprietor, who explains that the museum is dedicated to artefacts collected from criminal acts. The final exhibit she is shown involves a holographic image of a man, Clayton Leigh. The proprietor explains that before Leigh's execution for murder, his consciousness was downloaded from his brain, generating this hologram, which can respond to others and feel pain. The hologram is used as a simulation of Leigh's execution. Visitors are encouraged to press a switch, which electrocutes him, forcing the simulation to suffer time and time again. Visitors can then download the data from the electrocution into a key ring to take home, capturing the hologram's agony in perpetuity as a grisly souvenir. It is eventually revealed that the woman is Leigh's daughter. She takes revenge on the proprietor by treating him as he treated her father.

All of these *Black Mirror* episodes (and several others across the four seasons) are suffused with the affective forces and agential capacities of people's digitized information. They vividly and imaginatively demonstrate the nightmarish ways in which personal data can be used to monitor, frighten, humiliate, punish and even torture people, particularly in imagined scenarios when digital devices can be used to constantly record, preserve, download and revisit these data. Like Frankenstein's monster, these personal data are portrayed as new forms or extensions of human life. More than data doubles or doppelgängers, these personal data have their own liveliness, their own social worlds, that exist beyond the control of the humans who created them.

It is notable that a recent article in the *Guardian* (Smith 2018) employed the neologism of 'Franken-algorithms' to describe what its headline described as 'the deadly consequences of unpredictable code'. The author, Andrew Smith, provided examples such as a self-driving car striking and killing a pedestrian in Tempe, Arizona, and the use of algorithms for high-frequency trading on the stock market which had gone 'rogue'. Smith referred to the impact of machine learning on automated decision-making as resulting in humans having no knowledge or control over how algorithms are developed or their effects. These are the 'Franken-algorithms': human creations that have escaped the control of their creators.

These kinds of popular representations of personal data and their consequences go some way to highlighting the uncanny and potentially uncontrolled – and in some cases, disastrous – implications of generating and storing personal data. In their more-than-human presence, they have the potential to evoke the 'uncanny valley', or the affective response humans can have to objects they have created that is marked by feelings of eeriness, uncertainty and a sense that something is 'not quite right' (Mori et al. 2012). Humanoid robots are often described as evoking uncanny valley responses, but they can occur in response to other digital as well as non-digital humanoid artefacts, such as masks, dolls, puppets, zombies, human prosthetics, characters in films generated by computer graphic manipulation (sometimes referred to as 'digital actors') and avatars in computer games (Geller 2008). From the ambivalence of the uncanny valley to the monstrosities of data betrayals, the near-future of personal data is imagined in unsettling scenarios. Crucially, however, in most of these scenarios, it is other humans who use people's personal data against them. The digital tools are simply convenient routes by which humans' inhumanity to other humans can be achieved.

The less disturbing dimensions of these data portrayals refer to the creepiness that third-party use of personal data can arouse. 'Creepy' is an adjective that is increasingly often used in popular cultural references to dataveillance (Tene and Polonetsky 2013b). In 2014, for example, the *Guardian* published an article headlined 'When data gets creepy: the secrets we don't realise we're giving away' (Goldacre 2014). The author drew attention to the types of personal information that online interactions were collecting and leaking to third parties.

> Information we have happily shared in public is increasingly being used in ways that make us queasy, because our intuitions about security and privacy have failed to keep up with technology. Nuggets of personal information that seem trivial, individually, can now be aggregated, indexed and processed. When this happens, simple pieces of computer code can produce insights and intrusions that creep us out, or even do us harm. (Goldacre 2014)

In a more recent example, a *Sydney Morning Herald* story on the ways in which the Apple Map's app on iPhones tracks users' movements and geolocation was headlined 'Dear Apple, while we're talking about creepy data collection …' (Hanna 2018). The author, Conal Hanna, remarked that even though he never used Apple Maps, preferring the Google Maps app for finding directions, the Apple Map app sent him regular notifications. One notification had made mention of his small daughter's childcare service by name, and this particular detail had aroused Hanna's disquiet:

> Here is an app that I don't use that knows not only where my daughter goes to day care, but seemingly what days she goes and roughly what time we are taking her there … I don't know about you, but I find that creepy. (Hanna 2018)

Hanna went on to take Apple CEO Tim Cook to task for proclaiming that his company was not interested in data-profiling their customers. As Hanna noted, his smartphone software must have gathered data from various sources on his phone and processed them algorithmically to conclude that he had a young daughter who went to a certain childcare service on certain days. He had noticed that in the Maps settings, it is stated that Siri (personal assistant software on Apple devices) can suggest locations based on the user's Safari and app usage. Hanna stated:

> I'm not paranoid enough to think Apple is using this data for nefarious Big Brother purposes. I think they're attempting to be useful with this traffic service – even though for me it never has been. But this data clearly could be used for inappropriate purposes. And permission for its collection definitely wasn't explicitly sought.

These news stories identify several elements of how internet companies' collection and processing of digitized personal information can be defined as creepy. First, the authors were initially unaware of the types of personal details the companies were curating and using. Second, it is not only personal data about users that are involved, but also potentially family members (such as Conal Hanna's young daughter). Third, these personal details can be used by third parties in ways of which the individuals concerned may have little or no knowledge and to which they may not have explicitly consented. And finally, these data may be combined to generate insights into users' lives and habits that they may previously not have realized themselves: in effect, 'giving away secrets'.

The affective force of creepiness involves a feeling of discomfort or disturbance, that something is 'not quite right', a visceral response of queasiness. This affective force shares some of the uncanny valley phenomenon, but is perhaps more mundane and has wider resonances beyond the technological/robotic. An acquaintance's behaviour can be experienced as creepy, for example, if she or he behaves in a way that flouts social norms and expectations: the person is too familiar, over-shares, invades one's personal space and so on. Creepiness brings vague dreads, fear or disgust into everyday places, spaces and social relations.

Julia Kristeva's concept of the abject (Kristeva 1982) is at play in the creepy affect. The abject is that human or nonhuman thing that arouses feelings of discomfort and disgust because it flouts cultural boundaries such as those routinely defined between human/nonhuman, Self/Other, female/male and inside/outside. In people's efforts to conceptually contain their bodies/selves to achieve the modern Western ideal of autonomy and individuation, they seek to expel the abject from their bodies/selves to try to make themselves clean, pure and bounded. Importantly, the abject person or thing can also inspire feelings of fascination and desire because of its unusual and norm-flouting ontological status. Ambivalence, therefore, is a strong element of abjection and creepiness, as people are simultaneously attracted to and repelled by the individual or object that is engendering these feelings.

Dirty data

Beyond the ways in which the exploitation of personal data can generate disturbing and unsettling affective forces, their production, storage and use can have material effects on human bodies and the environment. The construction and disposal of the digital devices used to generate digitized information and the massive data centres that are required to store this information demand high rates of energy and water use to function (Hogan 2018). 'Cloud' computing is far from being as ephemeral as the metaphor may suggest. Jussi Parikka (2012: 97) asserts that digital technologies possess 'weird materialities', as they 'remain irreducible to either their "hard" contexts and pollution (CO_2, toxic materials, minerals, and other component parts) or their "soft" bits (signs, meanings, attractions, desires)'. In all dimensions of the making, use and discarding of digital technologies, human bodies are implicated: and sometimes harmed (as when labourers in developing countries are exploited in making devices, and people living or working in areas where devices are recycled or discarded are exposed to their leaking toxins). Parikka refers to these kinds of encounters as generating 'dirty media': digital technologies that pose harms to the environment and to human bodies.

In these contexts, the agency of this digital matter can become harmful or reduce vitalities and potentialities of human–nonhuman assemblages. Another interpretation of 'dirty media', however, might be the ways in which personal digital data are leaked from devices or archives, which can then exert material effects on people. In the early 1990s, popular representations of computing began to employ the metaphor of computer 'viruses' to describe the ways in which people's computers could be 'invaded' and 'contaminated' by malicious software invented to adversely affect the operation of the computer. These programs could spread from computer to computer in those days principally by entering into networked computing systems or via email attachments. The computer virus metaphor represented computers as vulnerable living creatures that could be infected by another living organism that contaminated their bodily integrity and compromised their 'health' by introducing 'disease' (Lupton 1994). While computer viruses are still operational, a new form of anxiety about digital technologies focuses on the potential of people's personal data to be accessed via illegal activities from hackers or cybercriminals or even legally by internet companies and app developers. The metaphor of the digital technological system as a living entity has extended from the hardware and software to the data themselves. There is less emphasis on disease and infection, however, and a greater focus on employing cultural concepts of contamination.

The 'clean' and 'dirty' binary opposition is frequently employed to conceptualize digital and other forms of data. The terms 'clean' and 'dirty' have long been used in descriptions of data, however these data are generated. These terms refer to the degree to which the data can be used for analysis: clean data are ready for use, while dirty datasets require further processing to make them 'clean' enough to use. It is notable that discussions of how people should protect their personal data have begun to use the term 'data hygiene' to describe best practice. This phrase has been used for some years in data science circles to describe how data 'cleansing' should happen.

'Dirty' data originally referred to data that are corrupted, outdated, duplicated, incomplete or inaccurate in some way, and which needed work to restore them to a point where they could be useable for analytical purposes. Sometimes the term 'bad data' is used for these types of data. The headline of a blog post by a data science company encapsulates these meanings: 'Data hygiene: create a culture of cleanliness to beat bad data' (Neubarth 2013). Data have also been referred to as 'raw', suggesting that they are materials that are untouched by culture (Gitelman and Jackson 2013). It is assumed that by working on 'raw' data, data scientists transform these materials into useable commodities. Part of this transformation may involve 'cleaning' 'dirty data'. Boellstorff (2013) uses the term 'rotted data' to describe the ways in which the materiality of data can degrade so that it is no longer 'clean', but also how data can be transformed in unplanned or accidental ways that do not follow algorithmic prescriptions. These organic metaphors of 'raw', 'cooked' and 'rotted' draw attention to the materiality of data, highlighting their mutability and vulnerability, their lively capacities to decompose and recompose.

Concepts of dirt and cleanliness are culturally and historically dynamic. What matter is considered 'dirty' or 'clean' in a specific cultural and historical context is revealing of dominant norms and affects that are closely associated with ideas about embodiment, selfhood and social relations (Campkin and Cox 2012; Duschinsky 2013). The use of metaphors related to dirt and cleanliness is itself indicative of underlying fears and anxieties about loss of control and containment, of corruption and vulnerability. Hygiene rituals are directed at making people feel comfortable (Shove 2004): both in terms of their embodied sensations and their sense of wellbeing and security.

Mary Douglas's structural anthropological scholarship on dirt as 'matter out of place' can be brought to bear on the understanding of how personal data should be used and who should have access to them. Douglas (1966) argued that notions of purity and contamination are important in cultural frameworks of identifying Self and Other and maintaining symbolic boundaries between social groups. Dirty or contaminating things or people often are viewed as transgressing or blurring cultural boundaries, and therefore as anomalies, creating cultural anxieties and fear or even strong feelings of disgust and revulsion. They are positioned as Other to the Self. Such distinctions are often associated with moral codes. Those people, animals and or objects that are considered as 'impure' or 'dirty' are also often considered unlawful, wicked, wrong or threatening to human health or wellbeing, provoking indignation, censure or punishment.

'Dirty data' are details that are embarrassing, humiliating, that can be used against the person and make them feel uncomfortable. Exposing personal data to others is like exposing their secrets. The word that is often used when people discuss their concerns about where their personal data go and who may see them or reveal them is 'creepy'. This term suggests again a feeling of vulnerability, of being watched by an entity that has malevolent motives. Dataveillance and data exploitation are 'creepy' because people are uncertain exactly how they are taking place and feel that they lack control over the process because of its mysterious nature. They lie outside ordinary human perception and knowledge and are therefore unsettling. They are uncanny, involving strange and unknown elements within the familiar setting of the everyday.

Data materializations beyond the visual

The tools used to digitally generate and materialize personal data are by necessity reductive and normative, as well as generative. The ways in which certain phenomena are selected to become digital data and how these data are then stored and processed are part of the micropolitics of data. Digital technologies work to capture and materialize immanent dimensions of human embodiment and practices, creating human–data assemblages. Unlike previous forms of digitized bodily informatics, which were often confined to medical domains and trained experts, many novel digital technologies offer any interested person the opportunity to document, monitor and measure details of their bodies. Materializations of personal data are agential cuts. They work to 'freeze' lively data assemblages at a certain point in time and place, providing data objects that help people make sense of their personal information. These data objects represent a specific digital data assemblage that existed at the time of freezing – and then goes on to change again as more data points are generated and configured into new versions of the assemblage and as people engage with them and incorporate them into their everyday lives.

Many scholars have identified and examined what has been described as 'the visual turn' in Western cultures, involving the progressive move towards privileging sight and sound. Sight in particular, and to a lesser extent sound, have become valued and viewed as higher senses compared with the other three: touch, smell and taste, which are commonly represented as baser and more emotional, animalistic and instinctive (Paterson 2007; Classen 2012). In studies of the sovereignty of visuality, visual images are described as possessing significant power in representing and conveying social and cultural meaning. It has been contended that the development of photography and cinema films in the early twentieth century, in particular, contributed to conventions of representing and understanding the world and people using visual images (Jay 2002; Burri 2012).

This privileging of the visual is evident in the ways in which digital data are typically presented. The term 'data visualization' is commonly employed to refer to the manifestations of digital data that can be configured as visual objects. It is a sub-field of information visualization, which refers to representing any information visually. In human–computer interaction research, both information and data visualization design are directed at communication: specifically, facilitating people's understanding of and engagement with information (or, in human–computer interaction language, their 'processing' of the information). Data visualizations involve taking pieces of information and rendering these into visual formats, involving the mapping of this information onto a property such as shape, colour, size and position and arranging these properties in space so that they have a relationship to each other that is designed to convey the meaning of the information. These formats are most often two-dimensional images: charts, maps, graphs, infographics and other diagrams, some of which may be interactive, moving when clicked. A dominant expression in the data visualization community is that of 'beautiful data': a term that points directly to the importance to those who work in 'data viz' to produce spectacular and aesthetically pleasing images that not only communicate information clearly but do so in a visually arresting form (McCosker and Wilken 2014; Gregg 2015b; Kennedy et al. 2016; Kennedy and Hill 2017).

The visual is often implicated within multiple power relations: its power 'continues to challenge and be challenged by other ways of knowing', creating certain kinds of 'frictions', or dissonances, resistances and challenges (Frosh and Becker 2015). While the digitization of phenomena has emphasized in some ways their visual dimensions, these materializations of the digital are often 'in friction' with other modes of understanding and experience (Frosh and Becker 2015). Just as visual representations are enactments of tacit assumptions and embedded power relations (Burri 2012; Frosh and Becker 2015; Hill et al. 2016), any mode of sensory knowledge, including those other than the visual, are shaped via social, cultural and political processes. For instance, science and technology scholars have drawn attention to the ways in which visualizations of scientific data work to generate scientific knowledge in specific ways, constituting the research objects themselves. Conventions of representation operate, in which scientists learn to produce and interpret images as part of their working and scholarly communication cultures (Latour 1986; Burri et al. 2011).

Digitized representations of bodily processes and attributes work to simplify the complexities of human flesh and action at the same time as they selectively emphasize some details over others. When bodily processes are monitored by digital sensors and rendered into digital data, they are made visible in unprecedented ways. Elements of people's bodies and habits that they may not otherwise have considered to any great extent – the number of steps they take per day, their sleep patterns, the kilometres and geographical locations they move through, their brainwaves, moods and so on – are given a visual status and brought into sharp relief.

In these contexts, the body/self becomes a series of inter-relating digitized informatics, which demand new ways of interpreting these signs and signals of bodily function and movement and of self-identity. These visualizations are typically rendered as numbers or graphics on smart devices, and often ordered in such a way that changes over time can be noted. Because of the way they are constructed, our eye is drawn to notice a limited number of dimensions of our bodies, rendered in metric or graphical form.

While the visual materialization of data remains a dominant concern, a counter-trend in human–computer interaction studies and design literature focuses on the other senses and how they contribute to representations and understandings of data. A field of research that has emerged devotes attention to the ways in which data can be rendered into three-dimensional physical artefacts – commonly referred to as 'data physicalizations' – and how these data forms can support cognition, communication, learning, problem-solving and decision-making. The idea that multisensory experiences are richer and better under-stood than those that tend to emphasize only the visual dimension is evident in this literature. It is argued that such artefacts facilitate knowledge of data that otherwise would not be available by using such features appealing to haptic sensations as texture, stiffness, temperature and weight (Jansen et al. 2015; Stusak 2015).

As demonstrated by the 'Data Physicalization Wiki' (2019), human societies have rendered information into physical forms for millennia, including the clay tokens used by the Mesopotamians, the quipus or knotted ropes used by the Incas, and the Marshall Islanders' stick charts. More recent data physicalizations featured on this wiki involve the use of personal information that have been turned into tangible objects, including Andreas Nicolas Fischer's data sculptures made from data such as a week of mobile phone communications, Cory Imig's Lego block constructions demonstrating her travels around her city, a set of tableware based on personal data such as blood test results and coffee consumption by Iohanna Pani, and a physicalization using cigarette butts made by Giacomo Flaim to demonstrate the average annual cigarette consumption of Italian smokers.

Several human–computer interaction projects have used 3D-printing technologies as a method of inviting people to engage in the act of creating objects from their personal data. The idea of such work is to encourage reflection and conversations about the information and to help people feel as if they have more control of and engagement with their personal data by allowing them to make their own artefacts. If these acts of fabrication take place in a communal setting, they may become less individualized, resulting in shared and social experiences of generating personal data physicalizations. For example, Nissen and Bowers (2015) have experimented with encouraging people to engage in 'data making' by producing 'data-things' from their own data. These physical data representations become personal data artefacts. Nissen and Bowers refer to such activities as 'participatory data translation'. Such digital data physicalizations, they argue, are experienced as less 'alien' than mass-produced things because their makers have better knowledge of how they are fabricated and they have a far more personal provenance. One example of these data-things is the objects that were created from the tweets generated by attendees at a conference. The number of tweets using the conference hashtag created by each attendee over a period of twenty-four hours was fabricated into an object that could be worn as a broach representing the extent of that person's Twitter engagement. The researchers argue that through engaging in this process of data translation, participants can gain a sense of the reconfigurations that data undergo. The liveliness of the data becomes more evident (Nissen and Bowers 2015).

The growing cultural resonances of personal data practices are becoming expressed in artistic and craft-based responses. A range of creative expressions of and challenges to personal data has been exhibited or displayed on artists' websites.

Self-described US-based 'data artist' Laurie Frick works to use personal data in artistic ways that highlight their richness and affective force, generating 'data-portraits'. For Frick, this approach avoids the creepiness of personal data by emphasizing its value for creativity and self-insight (Frick 2019). Frick has experimented with a range of materials to materialize personal data in three-dimensional artefacts. One of her latest artworks, *Felt Personality*, used colourful pieces of wool felt she had hand-dyed. The felt pieces were cut, coloured and positioned to present data from the dating app OKCupid. Another artwork, *Acrylic Friends*, involved the use of colourful transparent acrylic blocks, listing every person who has had some kind of influence on Frick throughout her life. The piece began as a computer spreadsheet with the details about these people listed by Frick, noting what she remembers about them and how they have influenced her. These details were then printed on the acrylic blocks, for display in stacks arranged by Frick to represent their collective influence over her lifetime (these artworks can be viewed on Frick's website: https://www.lauriefrick.com/).

Other artists have sought to emphasize the ways in which nonhuman objects can intra-act with human bodies in personal data experiments. Tega Brain's *Smell dating* (2019) invites people to select potential romantic partners by responding to a piece of fabric infused with their body odours. Luke Munn's *Domestic data* (2019) uses the contents of a home vacuum cleaner filter bag as data that can reveal patterns of activity of the home's inhabitants (including pets). Tyler Fox's (2018) work focuses on highlighting the ways in which nonhuman organisms can be employed to visualize human data. His *Biolesce* project involved bioluminescent algae that emitted flashes of intense blue light in response to human heartbeats tracked by digital sensors. In his interactive installation, human participants could watch the algae pulse in time to their own heartbeats, emphasizing the more-than-human relationship between these biological entities. The *Conflict Sculptures* created by Jill Miller's art-making participants used the medium of colourful play dough (Miller 2018). The participants, all parents of young children, made play dough balls and placed them in sculptural configurations to represent incidents and the intensity of angry outbursts at home by each family member. Craft methods such as weaving, knitting and cooking have also been taken up to explore the potentials of portraying data using a range of unconventional materials. In their *Data Cuisine* project (2018), members of the German art and design collective Prozessagenten use food to materialize data. As the website header puts it, 'What is the taste of data?' (Data Cuisine 2018). Drawing on open data sources, the collective configures recipes to present the data as a series of tastes and textures. In a workshop the collective ran in Switzerland, for example, the *Onionland* piece presented food made with onion layers and different kinds of edible fillings to represent the percentage of the population who used the internet browser Tor for anonymous internet access. Another data cuisine dish, *Zuckerberg Pops*, presented data about the percentages of people in Arab Spring nations who use Facebook, in the form of cake pops with different types of sprinkles to represent the statistics. A further effort to materialize personal data in edible form involved the use of Australian census statistics on the ethnic ancestry of residents of twelve Sydney suburbs that featured a dominant ethnic group (Tatham 2018). A data analyst worked with a professional chocolatier to compose recipes for chocolates that included signature flavours from the countries that were most highly represented in several suburbs. For example, a chocolate was created representing a suburb with a high proportion of residents from an Indian background with components such as cardamom, coconut and cashew, while the Chinese ancestry of residents in another suburb was represented in a chocolate featuring the flavours of red bean, coconut and mandarin.

Speculative and critical data materializations

Creative design- and arts-based approaches to personal data can begin to reveal the more-than-representational dimensions of data assemblages, particularly the affective and sensory aspects that may be difficult to articulate in conventional modes of academic writing or research. Beyond these approaches to data materialization lies a further opportunity for design- and arts-based methods to uncover the social and political dimensions of personal data practices and cultures. Cultural critics often call for new stories to be imagined and told when conceptualizing the futures of science and technology: Haraway calls this 'speculative fabulation' (Franklin and Haraway 2017).

One source of new and alternative fabulations are artists, creative writers and designers who have engaged in projects that seek to challenge taken-for-granted assumptions about personal digital data. These works draw attention not only to the liveliness of human–data assemblages, but also the capacities they can generate for reinvention, exploitation and deterioration. Speculative design involves configuring future imaginaries that may not be expected to come to pass (Dunne and Raby 2013). Unlike some design approaches, therefore, it is not directed at problem-solving, but rather at problematizing futures. By inspiring or responding to speculative design artefacts and ideas, participants are provoked into thinking differently and creatively, raising questions about conventions and assumptions. Speculative design methods can also uncover the rationales and meanings behind what might be considered to be unusual, irrational, unexpected or perverse uses of objects, and in doing so, contribute to new ways of thinking about their possibilities as well as their deficiencies (Lupton and Michael 2017; Lupton 2018c).

Using speculative design, researchers have invented objects that are meant to provoke imaginative and unsettling responses to personal data. Thus, for example, as part of *Persuasive Anxiety*, a project seeking to investigate self-tracking, Gross and colleagues (2017) invented three artefacts that were designed to be controversial. These devices were made to be deliberately intrusive as a way of foregrounding the performative nature, anxiety-inspiring qualities and privacy implications of collecting self-tracked data for health and behaviour change. Participants in their study were asked to use the devices over a period of six months in their homes, with the researchers meeting regularly with them to interview them about their experiences and conducting observations of how the devices were used. The researchers were interested in how these devices worked to defamiliarize and disrupt conventional assumptions about self-tracking technologies, opening up new ideas about how these technologies might be employed in everyday life.

A small body of literature has begun to be developed by scholars who take critical approaches to data visualization. Writers who have contributed to this literature have insisted on approaching data visualizations as politically charged phenomena that are the products of and serve to reproduce tacit assumptions, knowledge and power relations. They contend that data visualization is a form of ideological knowledge production, in which certain elements are chosen to be manipulated in specific ways to create and emphasize relationships while others are ignored or underemphasized. Powerful interests and existing biases and discrimination are frequently reproduced as part of the decisions made in creating data visualizations (D'Ignazio 2015; Kennedy et al. 2017; Kennedy and Hill 2018).

As feminist critics and others have contended, such visualizations often tend to be accepted as politically neutral and value-free (D'Ignazio 2015; Hill et al. 2016). Little attention is paid to where the information that is represented in such aesthetically pleasing images comes from, who collects it, how accurate it is and whose interests it serves. The decisions made about what data are included and which are not, and indeed, what features even count as data, for example, are elided in most data visualizations. Like other popular-culture artefacts, data visualizations can work to stigmatize, marginalize and trivialize disempowered social groups.

Some of the most interesting critical work related to data visualizations has come from feminist critics of geographic information systems. They have challenged the positivist scientific practices and assumptions of this method of mapping and called for alternative practices that highlight injustices and inequalities, such as 'counter-mapping', or generating cartographic representations that challenge taken-for-granted assumptions and highlight aspects that previously were not visible (e.g., Kwan 2002; Elwood 2008). In some cases, such counter-mapping involves the use of material other than two-dimensional visual images. For example, feminist geographer Mei-Po Kwan (2002) used 3D digital mapping technologies to generate what she describes as 'body maps' of women, portraying their movements as life paths in three-dimensional space and comparing these maps with those of women of different socio-economic status and ethnicity. Other feminist geographers have employed qualitative rather than quantitative data in geographic information systems by adding voices and other sounds, hand-drawn images, photographs and videos, seeking to display and emphasize the richness of information that lies outside numerical data (Pavlovskaya 2006).

For some artists, their collection, interpretation and display of personal data are driven by the desire not to collect and display 'truthful' data, but rather to reflect on the practice and its implications for concepts of the self and the body. These kinds of artworks are attempts to portray personal data in multisensory, unconventional and surprising ways. In so doing, the artists work towards expanding the definition of personal data well beyond the accepted idea of these details as numerical or digitized. For example, members of the Museum of Random Memory, a collective of academics, artists and activists based in Denmark, have experimented with various ways of reflecting on the materiality and more-than-representational elements of everyday digital media use, including personal data. The collective focuses on performative arts-based public interventions to stimulate thinking and critique. The *Glitch Memory* (Light et al. 2018) intervention was an interactive museum experience, where visitors 'donated' memories which were then displayed as a performative attempt to represent these archives of memories as a resource for future archaeologists. In one example, a digital video of an elderly Danish woman recounting memories of her experiences in wartime Jutland was deliberately 'glitched', or tampered with, and displayed in the exhibition to encourage audiences to consider how such digitized memories can be corrupted or decompose and the implications for archiving memories.

Another intervention by this collective, *The Sound of Forgetting* (O'Connor et al. 2018), asked questions about personal details that are not archived, and therefore are lost. These details may be sensory embodied memories that are not captured by orthodox methods of recording human experience, such as digitized data. Or they may be memories that are deliberately not recorded because they are transgressive in some way, or because they are not considered important enough to be recorded and stored in public archives. Some potentially archivable material portraying human experience may be deliberately destroyed, degraded or discarded, or lost because of accidental damage. The artists observe that some digital data are themselves readily lost to the archive, because they are so lively and ephemeral or difficult to record or recover. They give the example of a Twitter conversation, involving several tweets and responses to tweets. The artists note that 'the meaning of this tweet series is diffuse, perhaps ineffable. It's not an archivable object, but more a swirl of constantly emerging information, which in turn morphs the reading of the story' (O'Connor ct al. 2018). They contend that these reflections have implications for how we think about digitized personal data in a context in which citizens are encouraged to believe that data archives record everyone's details for perpetuity.

Intensifying the affective forces of digitized information can also serve to provoke people into responding more viscerally to issues concerning what happens to their personal digital data. The affective responses that data physicalizations can evoke may lead people to engage more actively, including at the political level, in challenges to violations of their personal data privacy and security (Stark 2016). Some artists have employed 3D printing technologies as part of their critique of the ways in which personal data can be used for surveillance purposes. In her artwork *Stranger Visions* (2019), Heather Dewey-Hagborg took digital genetic data files, turned them into phenotypes (the physical manifestations of genomic data) and then printed out data sculptures of human heads based on the genetic data. She used cast-off objects that she had found in public places to derive the DNA traces: masticated chewing gum wads, fallen strands of hair, cigarette butts or fingernail clippings. The point of this artwork was to emphasize the extent and range of the detailed information that can now be collected about people, right down to their genetic profiles, and the inferences that can be made about them using these details. This work was designed to be a stark reminder to people of how their bodily traces can be datafied and used for the purposes of others, possibly revealing their identities or other sensitive information in the process.

Several other artists and arts collectives have produced works that emphasize the politics of data and algorithmic governance. In an artwork intended to critique the exploitation of human bodies for profit, the Institute of Human Obsolescence (2019) team asked participants to wear clothing embedded with sensors to harvest the heat from their bodies. The heat generates electricity, which is then transformed into cryptocurrency. In a similar project, British artist Max Dovey's *Respiratory Mining* (2019) uses human respiration to mine cryptocurrencies. Dovey employs this concept as a provocation to consider the ways in which a human bodily capacity – breath – can generate digital data, which in turn can become a universal currency, algorithmically processed to generate commercial value on digital systems such as the blockchain.

American artist Jennifer Lyn Morone (2018) has critiqued the commodification of personal data by turning herself into an 'incorporated person' (entitled 'Jennifer Lyn Morone, Inc.'). In a satirical explanation of her artwork, she claims on her website that by collecting as much information about themselves as possible, individuals can increase their commercial value:

> Jennifer Lyn Morone, Inc has advanced into the inevitable next stage of Capitalism by becoming an incorporated person. This model allows you to turn your health, genetics, personality, capabilities, experience, potential, virtues and vices into profit. You are the founder, CEO, shareholder and product using your own resources.

In an art project addressing the ephemerality of personal data, the members of the panGenerator studio developed an interactive installation, *hash2hash – Everything Saved Will Be Lost* (2019) for the National Ethnographic Museum in Warsaw. The installation invited visitors to take a selfie and load it onto the large installation screen. They looked on as the digital image of themselves gradually deteriorated, the screen emitting real flakes of ash that fall to make a pile around a tombstone inscribed with the hashtag symbol. The idea of this exhibition was to encourage visitors to reflect on their mortality and the limited lifespan of their personal data. Other artists' work has sought to draw attention to the potentially repressive nature of dataveillance technologies. For example, one of the pieces by US-based artist Zach Blas, entitled *Face Cages* (2018), shows people wearing metal masks that have been designed to look like the biometric visualization diagrams used in facial recognition software. Worn over the face like cages, the masks represent facial recognition as confining of human agency, individuality and identity. With *Face Cages*, Blas also seeks to draw attention to the limitations of facial recognition software and other forms of digital biometric applications in identifying people whose bodies are non-normative: non-whites, transgendered people and those with disabilities, for example. As Blas notes on his website:

> These diagrams are a kind of abstraction gone bad, a visualization of the reduction of the human to a standard, ideological diagram. When these diagrams are extracted from the humans they cover over, they appear as harsh and sharp incongruous structures; they are, in fact, digital portraits of dehumanization. (Blas 2018)

The *Algorithmic History Museum* was a pop-up exhibition curated by Ellen Bijsterbosch and Casper de Jong working with artists Milou Backx, Sosha de Jong and Sophie Pluim (Wieringa 2018). The exhibition, displayed in Eindhoven, the Netherlands, drew from three examples from Dutch history to present fictionalized algorithmic 'solutions' to historical 'problems' as a way of provoking reflection on these solutions' contemporary manifestations. Thus, for example, a 'what if' scenario involved African slaves captured by Dutch traders in the eighteenth century. Many of the slaves died en route to the Netherlands due to the appalling living conditions on the vessels in which they were imprisoned. The fictional 'solution' proposed in the exhibition is for the slaves to wear bracelets that track their exercise, algorithmically processed to allow for the slavers to monitor the slaves' health. The contemporary analogy is that of third parties exploiting for profit the data generated by people wearing digital devices to track their health indicators, and questions the privacy of these data and coercion to wear them (e.g., by employers or health insurance companies).

Summary

In this chapter, I have discussed a number of different ways in which personal data have been conceptualized and materialized in popular culture and also considered some design- and arts-based provocations. As I have shown, the onto-ethico-epistemological status of personal data constantly shifts in popular representations between human and nonhuman, valuable commodity and waste matter, nature and culture, productive and dangerous. The agential capacities of human–data assemblages – their ceaseless production, movements, leakages – are portrayed as both exciting and full of potential but also as dangerous and risky. Personal data assemblages are represented as difficult to control or exploit by virtue of their liveliness but also as offering greater insights than any other information source about people, to such an extent that they can be disturbing in their challenging of human privacy and integrity. The next chapter considers how people work to make sense of their personal data and incorporate these details into their concepts of selfhood and embodiment.

4

Doing Data

The vitality of personal data presents a great challenge to growing and learning with them. Digital data assemblages are dynamic, responsive and distributed forms of selfhood; because of their mutable nature, they are elusive, hard to pin down and manage. In this chapter, I address this issue of 'doing data': the performances, enactments and sense-making work in which people engage as they respond to and incorporate their data into their lives, as they enact their data selves.

Data sense

The capacities of personal data assemblages to instigate learning and knowing are often championed, whether by people learning about their bodies and lives to optimize themselves, teachers drawing on learning analytics to discern how well students are absorbing and understanding information, commercial enterprises generating more detailed insights into consumer behaviours, employers determining how to maximize worker productivity, or researchers seeking to exploit big medical datasets to better understand patterns of illness and disease. Just as digital data assemblages consist of specific information points about people's lives, and thus learn from people as algorithmic processes manipulate this personal information, people in turn can potentially learn from their data. The products or potential dating partner choices that Amazon and OkCupid offer, the ads that are delivered to users on Facebook or Twitter, the returns that are listed from search engine queries or browsing histories, the information that fitness trackers provide about users' heart rate or calories burnt each day, are all customized to the users' digitized behaviours and preferences. Perusing these data can provide people with insights about themselves and may structure their future behaviour. People are confronted with making sense of the information, deciding how valid or valuable it is, and what to do with these details.

These engagements are often referred to in terms of 'literacy'. The data literacy discourse draws mainly on literatures in informatics, education and information literacy research, using the analogy of literacy as the ability to read: that is, understand and use text. Information is usually represented as material that is translated from thought to matter and back again to thought (Buckland 1991). In information studies, the concept of data literacy is closely related to that of information literacy. It refers to the ways in which people engage with and learn from information (Frank et al. 2016; Wolff et al. 2016). For example, in their definition, Wolff and colleagues (2016: 15) describe data literacy skills as 'abilities to select, clean, analyse, visualize, critique and interpret data, as well as to communicate stories from data and to use data as part of a design process'.

Despite personal data becoming increasingly generated by, on and with the human body, the interplay between the human senses and the digital sensors that work to document the body rarely receives attention. The fleshly, intuitive and sensory dimensions of these engagements are often ignored, in favour of the rationalist processes of human cognition and the materiality of nonhuman infrastructures. People using information systems are typically considered as atomistic actors, while the sociocultural and enfleshed dimensions of these systems are rarely addressed (Yoo 2010; Fors et al. 2013; Avital et al. 2017). It is only very recently in management and organizational studies, as well as the related fields of information systems and information studies, that new materialism perspectives have begun to emerge, particularly in relation to understanding humans' engagements with digitized information systems such as databases (Cecez-Kecmanovic et al. 2014). For example, Orlikowski and Scott (2008; 2015) draw on Barad's agential realism theory to propose an approach to sociomateriality in organizations and systems that sees meaning, humans and these systems as conceptually and materially inseparable.

Rather than refer to data literacy or data management skills, I prefer to use the term 'data sense' to encapsulate a broader meaning that acknowledges the role of fleshly and affective bodily affordances in people's responses to data, and also the role played by digital sensors in the act of 'sense-making'; or coming to terms with an understanding of digital data and incorporating it into notions of selfhood, embodiment and social relations. As the French philosopher Merleau-Ponty (1962; 1968) reminds us, we are embodied subjects and experience the world through our bodies and our senses. Our experiences and our judgements are always part of our 'being-in-the-world'. For Merleau-Ponty, 'being-in-the-world' is always intersubjective. Our embodiment is inevitably interrelational and intercorporeal. We experience the world as fleshly bodies, via the sensations and affective forces configured through and by our bodies as they relate to other bodies and to the affordances of material objects and spaces. We respond to these bodies and objects with all our senses, and this is essential to human experience, social relations and knowing our worlds.

The concept of data sense, as I seek to develop it, brings the body back in, acknowledging that we learn in and through our bodies. It incorporates the entanglements of the digital sensors with the human senses in the process of sense-making. In these enactments, bodies are not only knowing and perceiving (Latimer 2008), but they are sensing, responding to and assessing the information returned by digital sensors. I argue that data sense is key to how people enact their lively data and the agential capacities that emerge. This is a new conceptual approach that moves well on from ideas of data literacy and builds on the work of scholars like Orlikowski and Scott to acknowledge the more-than-human worlds and embodied dimensions of human–data assemblages. It strives to highlight the distributed and dynamic nature of subjectivity and embodiment that feminist new materialism perspectives emphasize. Data sense, therefore, may be conceptualized as the co-constitution of human and nonhuman sense-making, and this sense-making as one of the integral agential capacities that are intra-acted in and through data selves.

Human–data assemblages create new configurations of affordances. As I explained in chapter 1, a distributed and relational understanding of affordances positions them as more-than-human as people come together with their technologies. This expanded notion of affordance goes to the feminist new materialist interest in relational agencies and capacities. From this perspective, data are always part of the humans who claim to 'discover' and 'analyse' them. Rather than seek neutrality and scientific objectivity – to remove human 'bias' – from data, they are viewed as ways to make certain agential cuts to achieve insights, as materialisms that create experiences at the same time as they seek to represent these experiences (Barad 2007; St Pierre 2013; Koro-Ljungberg et al. 2017). Human–data assemblages generate relational connections, affective forces and agential capacities. From this approach, data can never be 'objective' or 'unbiased', as positivist researchers often claim.

Adopting a similar perspective on data selves acknowledges their more-than-human relational and mutually constitutive ontologies. Any attempt to define a thing as 'information' involves the performance of an agential cut. Making and learning can be viewed as forms of agential capacities generated from the intra-actions between things in assemblages. Knowing, as Barad (2003) puts it, is one body making itself intelligible to another body. These human–data assemblages are configured within broader networks and environments which again are mutually articulated and co-constitutive. People can make decisions from the constantly changing choices available about what words they use to describe phenomena and what material practices they engage in to generate or interact with phenomena.

Scholars working in early childhood studies and education have been particularly prominent in using feminist new materialism together with post-qualitative methods of enquiry to research the ways in which people learn about the world from a more-than-human perspective. Some of these researchers have devoted particular attention to how they enact their own research data as a form of information (Koro-Ljungberg et al. 2017). For example, Hillevi Lenz Taguchi (2012: 265) has taken up Barad's work to discuss the ways in which she engages with her research data. Lenz Taguchi emphasizes that research data do not 'speak for themselves' (Lenz Taguchi 2012: 270). Researchers must work to turn these data into coherent narratives, which are always inevitably partial and selective. Adopting a diffractive approach, she refers to research as 'a becoming-with data', involving 'transcorporeal engagements' in which the researcher is sensitized to the different embodied ways in which she interacts with and makes sense of her data (see also Hultman and Lenz Taguchi 2010). Lenz Taguchi discusses how diffractive analysis involves the researcher engaging in transcorporeality, acknowledging that the research data are entangled with the research/researcher inextricably. She asserts that:

> When reading diffractively, I want to read *with* the data, understanding it as a constitutive force, working with and upon me in the event of reading it ... This is about the uncovering of a reality that already exists among the multitude of realities already being enacted in an event. (Lenz Taguchi 2012: 274–5, emphasis in the original)

This process involves making data intelligible and knowable: organizing and ordering them in a particular way, sometimes involving affective responses to the vibrancy of data that cannot be easily described. The researcher's previous embodied and affective experiences contribute to her decisions about which data to select and how to configure data narratives so that they make sense to her and her audiences.

While Lenz Taguchi is here discussing her approach to diffractively analysing research data, the same perspective can be adopted to understand how people enact their data selves. Diffractive analysis draws attention to events and encounters of humans and nonhumans with each other that evoke transformation. These data both affect and are affected by the humans they make and remake. The person engaging with their data is a performative agent (Hultman and Lenz Taguchi 2010: 537) in an event with the data materializations, just as they earlier were agential in co-creating the data with the device they used to do this. As performative agents, individuals are actively engaging their bodies and minds as they are 'becoming-with data' (Hultman and Lenz Taguchi 2010: 538) and configuring their data selves. These are forms of lively imaginings and interpretings, in which knowing and being cannot be separated (Barad 2003).

How data come to matter

People engaging with their personal data often adopt a diffractive approach as they work to make sense of the data. This is facilitated by their personal investments in the data they are reviewing. The data are meaningful because they are about and for them. People recognize that these human–data assemblages offer them new insights into their bodies, habits and practices: insights that can, in turn, contribute to new forms of embodiment and selfhood.

My research with people who engage in self-tracking has found that this perspective on personal data is often expressed by people when they are explaining why they generate these data about themselves and what the value of the data are – in other words, how the data 'come to matter'. It is particularly when people become aware of ruptures and disjunctions when they are engaging in data sense that they move towards a more diffractive position. They start to engage in the work of articulating and making sense of their data and to identify what goes wrong or why these data don't work to help them in the ways they expect. People may also find that their data practices and sense-making bring them to a point where they can see alternative values and uses for the data or other ways to generate them or alternative sources of information that work better for them and feel more 'right'. Sensory engagements other than the visual can be important in this process.

In several of my research projects (see the Appendix for project details), many of the people involved were habituated self-trackers, who had successfully appropriated self-tracking practices into their everyday lives. I was interested in establishing how these individuals narrated and justified their use of self-tracking technologies and what their accounts reveal about their engagements with the social contexts and rationales underpinning self-tracking cultures. These questions help identify the agential capacities that enactments of self-tracking are able to generate, and which encourage people to continue to invest their time and effort in self-tracking practices.

The findings of these studies, analysed through the lens of feminist new materialism, surfaced many ways in which self-tracked data came to matter, as articulated in the participants' accounts. A wide variety of understandings of personal data were expressed. The 'data' the participants collected and reviewed included not only digitized metrics or graphs that appeared on smartphone apps or wearable devices from sensed bodily movements and functions, but also details they manually entered into computer spreadsheets or documents, emails, written numbers or words on paper, bank statements, diary entries, medical test results, readings on weight scales, and, less tangibly, the physical sensations or moods that were felt in their bodies.

Many participants who used apps or wearable devices for self-tracking described the ways in which these technologies afforded them insights that were otherwise imperceptible by their bodily sensory responses. The capacity to bring previously latent bodily processes into view and consciousness, and to connect these details to other elements of their lives, was a key motivator for participants' self-tracking work. The opportunity to easily record bodily functions and activities allowed them to uncover new forms of information about their bodies. People often referred to becoming 'more aware' of their bodies and how this awareness helped them manage aspects they found problematic. Apps and wearable devices could help with establishing and maintaining this awareness, but simple habits of taking notice of one's body and attempting to remember details from day to day were also commonly employed.

People's bodily sensory capacities were augmented and extended by the technological affordances of the apps and devices they used to become more aware of their bodies.

These capacities, in turn, led to positive feelings of motivation and accomplishment. Thus, for example, Patsy, who took part in my Australian Women and Digital Health project, described how she used an app to collect information about her physical activity and her response to the data:

> I found the app that monitored my steps really good because it gave me an idea of where I was going and it encouraged me to use it more and get up and do things more. Well, it was counting my steps, so it just gave me a general idea of how much I really was getting up and moving about and it encouraged me to move about more and sort of set myself goals.

Another participant in this study, Anna, described how she used a Samsung wearable device to track her sleep, body weight and heart rate. She noted that she reviews these data with other details she records about herself or just notes mentally, such as the medication she takes. Anna enjoys being able to compare the different metrics she records about her body and to note any relationships between these details and her other bodily capacities and sensations.

> I'm a bit of a data nerd. I just like seeing all those little correlations and then also the different types of medication, how that affects my behaviours as well ... Sometimes I'll put a note in my calendar to say, I started this medication here, started it there, finished it when, blah blah blah, then see if anything changes: specific hormones, oral contraceptives and stuff like that. I find that I have a very weird weight fluctuation with that, and also it does affect my sleep. That all just ties in as well.

The combination of digitized and non-technological approaches is demonstrated in the case of Matt, from my Australian Self-Trackers project, who reported that he is dealing with an anxiety condition. Matt said that he began monitoring his condition when his psychologist suggested he start becoming more aware of his moods and what factors influenced them. While he also uses a Fitbit to track his fitness, an app for financial tracking, a digital blood pressure monitoring device and digital scales for monitoring his weight, Matt tracks his moods and anxiety levels using his bodily capacities of awareness and memory. Matt said that he has attempted to develop awareness of his thoughts, moods and anxiety so that he is better sensitized to them:

> Moods and emotions, I guess I'm quite anxious, so I track it more often. So, if I'm feeling down for more than a few days I think what I can do about it. So that's sort of a little note in my head.

Matt said that for him, establishing a 'starting point', or a base figure that he can then compare his information against, is important to his digital self-tracking practices:

> I think the thing is, that at the point where you start, you then know where you're at. And then it's a matter of seeing, 'Okay what do I want to do with this?' For example, with the blood pressure, the normal range with the results. And then, think if I'm not in normal range what do I need to do about it ... And then track that in the app and see how you're progressing with that.

The participants in these studies often referred to biographical disruptions or ruptures in their lives, or times of transition and change, in which they looked to self-tracking practices and rationales to offer a way to manage change or chaos: typically, with the desire to identify patterns, achieve goals and improve their lives in some way. These events included turning 40 or 50, trying to conceive and starting to track fertility, becoming a parent, deciding to save money to reach a financial goal, or receiving a diagnosis of a significant health problem.

One example is David, who was part of the Australian Self-Trackers study. He said that he initially began monitoring his body as a preventive health measure, responding to a known family medical history: his mother has diabetes, and he wanted to avoid developing the disease himself. He was later diagnosed with sleep apnoea after realizing that he was waking each morning still feeling tired. Again, he has a family connection: his uncle has sleep apnoea. David also wanted to alleviate his sinusitis symptoms, so began tracking them in the attempt to identify what triggered the symptoms and how they could be relieved. His doctor told him that his high blood pressure could be related to his sleep apnoea. To avoid having to take medication, David chose to try using the apnoea monitoring machine as a way of determining how his sleep was being affected. There are therefore many compelling health-related reasons why David tracks all these elements of his body and his life, including his awareness of the potential risk of developing a serious condition due to his knowledge of his family history, as well as the current health problems he is trying to manage.

Maria was also interviewed as part of the Australian Self-Trackers study. She recounted several different life experiences that had contributed to her deciding to take up her current self-tracking practices. Maria first described how, as a teenager, she had begun helping her mother, who was struggling financially, to monitor her expenses. She said she had developed valuable financial-monitoring skills at that time that she has continued to practise: 'Well, it's mother nature to me, to keep an eye on finances, track my finances and stuff, 'cause I'm good at doing that.' Second, Maria talked about wanting to lose a great deal of weight, and how closely monitoring her weight and diet was an important part of trying to achieve that goal. Finally, she mentioned that her daughter has severe asthma. Maria said that she has had to learn to keep a close eye on her daughter's health and medication as part of caring for her: 'It's just something that you just know in your head you have to do it.' Maria said she is trying to teach her own two children to take a similar approach to their lives, 'so they can be very independent people'.

Another self-tracker, Michael, said that he began monitoring aspects of his body and life about nine years ago. He chose to do so for a number of different reasons. One important life event was the birth of his first child. Michael noted that he became aware of the importance of keeping a close eye on his spending now that he had a child to provide for. Then Michael developed arthritis and shoulder pain and decided that he needed to monitor his body and health closely to alleviate his conditions. His close focus on monitoring his water intake, for example, is linked to his arthritis, as he sees a relationship between the two: 'So I see water intake helping me be in control of other aspects of my body'. In Michael's responses, it was clear that for him, being in control, or more specifically, appearing to be doing everything to retain control, is very important to his sense of self, including his identity as a responsible and caring father: 'I need to assess all these things to gain control of what I am and who I am.' These participants' accounts suggested that the very act of self-tracking – their decision to 'take charge' of their lives by regularly monitoring themselves – was a profound act of selfhood and embodiment. They discussed the ways in which their practices generated the agential capacities of self-improvement, exerting control, identifying patterns, achieving goals, feeling better and being responsible. The broader sociocultural contexts in which monitoring of the body/self is undertaken were also revealed in the participants' accounts. The concept of the entrepreneurial, self-responsibilized citizen, espoused in popular imaginaries on self-tracking and 'the quantified self' (Lupton 2016b), was a dominant ideal in these people's accounts. The ways in which the participants described their self-tracking motivations and practices were strongly underpinned by concepts of morality, related to idealized concepts of selfhood and citizenship. Overwhelmingly, self-tracking was positioned as an autonomous, rational calculative practice, involving individual actors working to problematize, refine and improve their lives. As I discuss later in this chapter, however, there were also many affective forces that operated when these people were configuring their data selves.

The work of data sense

The scholarship of Ingold and Hallam (discussed in chapter 2) emphasizes the importance of making and articulating materials in ways that feel right, based on affective and sensory judgements of what works. These practices involve accumulated embodied learning and doing. My research on self-tracking as a set of emergent embodied and emplaced practices has found that the data generated were artefacts of both bodily knowledge and emotion, similarly produced through attentive labour – or what Hallam describes as 'articulation'. These metrics can tell people only limited details about their bodies. Just like a human bone in itself is meaningless, digital data by themselves mean nothing. They only make sense in the biographical contexts in which people decide to collect their data and the social relationships and cultural expectations, places and spaces in which they do so. Just as human bones and other artefacts are articulated as part of sense-making and moving through the world, so too are human–data assemblages.

Far from passively expecting machines to generate personal information that can then be meaningfully applied to their lives, self-trackers are agential, constantly engaging in the work of sense-making. The work of making, and making sense of, data involves people recognizing the resonances and accounting for the differences in these details: deciding if they 'feel right' (Pink and Fors 2017). Articulating one's personal data is a matter of connecting the metrics with the lived sensory and affective experiences of one's body and the other elements that are important in data sense-making. Articulation involves joining disparate pieces of information together to make an assemblage. Choices about articulation are context-based, and the worlds in which articulated data assemblages move are also contextual, drawing their meaning from these contexts and contributing to them as well. Experienced self-trackers know this, as they work to make sense of these data and incorporate them into their lives. They realize that they must improvise and provide context to the data – otherwise the information is meaningless. While some elements of self-tracking may be automated, what can never be left to the machines is the process of learning from one's data and drawing it into one's mundane routines, practices and performances of identity.

In my research with people who track their physical exercise, people often talked about trusting the 'numbers' that they see on the data visualizations that their app or other software provides them. They talked about not really 'knowing' how their bodies were responding to exercise until they glanced at their heart rate monitor while running or cycling or reviewed their data after their exercise. In many instances, these data were viewed as more 'truthful' or 'accurate' than the haptic and other sensations they felt from their bodies as they were exercising. However, in some cases, when people reviewed their data, they actively related them to the contexts in which they were generated and drew on their past experiences of tracking to determine how 'truthful' these details are. The validity of these data was not necessarily always accepted.

In the Self-Tracking Cyclists project, the participants engaged in digital monitoring of their bodies or their bicycles or both. These data were configured and interpreted via the material features of the spaces in which they rode their bikes, the human and nonhuman actors in these spaces, and features of the space such as the climatic conditions. When these cyclists were producing digitized information about their rides using technologies such as smartphone apps, wearable devices like a Garmin smartwatch, cycling-tracking platforms such as Strava, or a bike computer attached to their bicycle, they were contributing to a spatial-technological environment in which their movements through space were digitally monitored as well as aspects of their bodies' responses. The actions generated biometrics such as heart rate, energy expended and exercise intensity level, as well as details related to the geolocation of their trips, speed and kilometres travelled.

This study found that the cyclists reviewed data about their rides bearing in mind such factors as the weather conditions (e.g., how hot or windy it was during the ride), the traffic conditions, the behaviours of other road or cycle path users, other animals in the landscape (such as dogs running in front of their bicycles or birds swooping them), whether they were nursing an injury or getting over a cold and how accurate the GPS system was in the areas they were riding in. Each process of reviewing their data included consideration of some of these factors when people were deciding how valuable, important or accurate the metrics and other data materializations were that their devices or apps delivered to them. Sometimes the data were considered to be useless, because they failed to register the correct location of the user, or they did not properly sync to an app or platform, or because the monitoring device was unable to register and take account of how tired the user was from a bad night's sleep. In other cases, the data were considered helpful and useful, based on factors such as the participants' previous experiences of the ride and the data generated from previous rides, and how well the data accorded with their bodily sensations and memories of the trip.

The ways in which personal data are materialized on people's devices are an important technological affordance. For example, the data visualization properties that Strava offered Tony, a participant in the Self-Tracking Cyclists project, were key elements he used to compare all the details he collected about his cycle trips and easily see whether he had improved or how well he was riding compared with other users. Tony observed that he enjoyed reviewing the details that Strava provides to him about his rides: including gradient graphs, speed graphs, heart rate fluctuation graphs, and 'Power Zones', which provide a calculation based on combined data on heart rate, gradient and speed. He also enjoyed looking at the dashboard on his Garmin bike computer during his trips, so that he could monitor his data in real time.

Tony only had a short commuting ride but engaged in much longer trips on his leisure cycles. He paid particular attention to his heart rate readings during recreational rides (but not on his short commuting trip) to determine how much load he was putting on his body and to 'see if I am struggling'. On his commutes, Tony focuses mainly on the ride time information. He observed that the digital data he collected do shape how he felt about his body, 'because you are trying to use metrics to change something about it'. However, he was also aware that the data from his devices could only tell him so much. His devices, for example, could not determine that he was feeling tired from a bad night's sleep or because he had already completed a long ride that week, or that he was feeling unwell, or had had too many drinks the previous night, or that a knee injury was playing up. The algorithms on his software did not incorporate such elements of place as the air temperature or wind strength into their calculations of how far or fast he had ridden.

The spatial elements of the landscapes through which cyclists ride also contributed to the affordances of their practices. These elements were integral to the sensory and affective intensities that are part of the self-tracking cycling experience. For example, Ernie said that he recognized the sensation of when he is travelling quickly on his bicycle, but he liked to be 'accurate' by using the bike computer. He used the computer to 'confirm' how he was feeling: if he thought he was going slowly or quickly, the computer let him know if this was correct. In contrast, Damon preferred not to check his Garmin watch during his trips, as he wanted to ascertain by 'feel' how the ride was progressing. He observed that accumulated bodily experience of cycling helped him to make this kind of assessment:

> After you've been training for a number of years, you do get to know, gauge how you feel and what kind of effort you're putting in. It can be a bit surprising when you actually measure it versus how you feel. Sometimes you can be going a lot quicker than you thought, or you think you're riding fairly easy but you're actually going fairly quick. And other times, you're putting in a lot of effort but you're actually quite fatigued and you're actually not going that quick. I found it's good having the watch as well to validate that feeling versus reality.

Damon's strategy of waiting until later to check his data was also part of his desire to ensure that he cycled safely in dangerous conditions rather than trying to beat his times and therefore taking risks. Damon had made the decision to rely on his senses rather than the information provided by his digital sensors during cycle trips, including using previous experience to interpret how his body was responding to the conditions of the ride. His desire to exercise caution and avoid risk-taking also contributed to this decision. Yet once he was able to review his digital data, his sensory and experiential embodied knowledges were mediated by what these data revealed to him about the trip.

The details cyclists collected about their rides offered a further dimension to the sensory knowledges that their bodies bestowed. These data were conceptualized as providing greater detail and a type of quantified information that was beyond the capacity of the fleshly body. However, this was a complex, contingent and emergent interaction in practice. The participants interpreted their bodies partly via the digital data they generated and partly via their physical sensations and affects, often moving back and forth between these sources of data in making sense of their bodies' feelings and interpreting the meaning of their data.

The complexity and sheer hard work of self-tracking in situations where an individual is attempting to manage a chronic health condition is highlighted in Barbara's account of her practices. Barbara, a participant in the Australian Self-Trackers project, has type 1 diabetes, diagnosed six months prior to the interview. Even before this diagnosis, Barbara had been feeling generally unwell, and started using a wearable device and app to monitor her physical activity levels about eighteen months beforehand. Once she had been diagnosed, her doctor suggested that she track her diet, and Barbara uses a paper food diary for this. She was also provided with a blood glucose monitoring device.

In her interview, Barbara explained the complexities of what she is tracking and how she tries to use the details these methods generate:

> I guess there's different reasons for each of them. With the stepper, it's just wanting to walk at least three times a week, 10,000 steps. That's what I aim to do at least three times a week. With the food diary, what I need to do is to check if what I'm eating is affecting my blood sugars, I'm just watching what sugars have been triggering a high. So, I try to track the food to see if there's a correlation. And the device where I measure my blood, I just do that before the meal and two hours after the meal, and then I try to see if there's certain foods that I should avoid eating.

These studies revealed the extent of work required from people to enact their data: to learn the best methods for their purposes, to remember to continue them, and to make sense of and apply the information that was created. Even when personal data practices were automated by the use of apps and wearable devices, the people using them were far from passively allowing the devices to do the work for them. They were engaging in creative acts of data sense.

Data affects

Enactments of personal data are often suffused with intense affective forces. When people are reviewing the materializations of their data – images of themselves and others; social media updates or comments; or datasets showing details of their bodies, preferences and habits, such as those generated by self-tracking apps and devices – affective responses are often provoked. Interactions online with other people can also involve affective interchanges and responses. Posting images or videos, GIFs and memes, liking, commenting on or sharing other people's content and responding to others' comments and responses, can all be modes of affective exchange (Kuntsman 2012; Lupton 2019d). Affects are mediated, remediated and often amplified via intense interchanges that may involve many people. Indeed, the business model of social media is underpinned by their affordances of being able to attract and share emotional responses, thereby encouraging people to continually use them and to check how others are responding to their posts, updates and comments (van Dijck 2013; Kennedy 2016). This is part of the enchantments and thing-power of these technologies.

As discussed in chapter 3, data visualizations and other forms of data materializations are often manipulated by graphic designers and artists to encourage strongly sensory and affective responses in the effort to convey meaning and stimulate engagement. Kennedy and Hill's *Seeing Data* project focused in detail on the affective dimensions of data visualizations (Kennedy and Hill 2017; 2018). These researchers used the method of focus group discussions to invite English participants to respond to eight data visualizations, chosen to represent a cross-section that might be encountered in everyday life. The visualizations included a diversity of topics and approaches to materializing data. A smaller number of participants kept a diary recording their encounters with data visualizations for a month following the focus groups and were interviewed at the end of this month. The findings showed that the participants often responded emotionally to features of the visualizations such as the scale of the numbers represented and the visual style that was employed. Some expressed feelings of frustration or confusion in response to visualizations they found unclear or too simplistic. Other data visualizations evoked reactions such as anger, pleasure, sadness, guilt, shame, worry, relief, love, empathy and excitement.

My research has found that people often describe collecting and reviewing data about their bodies as generating agential capacities that are suffused with affect. I noted earlier in this chapter that the decision to take up self-tracking can be an affective response – a need to exert control over an unsettling or challenging experience or life change. Across the modes of monitoring and self-knowledge that my research participants were enacting, it was not only the metrics that people generated on themselves that were agential in their affective capacities. The very process of collection was itself meaningful in the comfort and sense of control it offered people. The participants referred to the benefits bestowed by becoming 'more aware' of their bodies and mental states. Their enactments of these practices bestowed agential capacities in and through bodies that were viewed as recalcitrant, but then were disciplined to be manageable and less chaotic.

Engagements with the data that are generated are also affectively charged. The self-trackers in my studies, for example, often described feelings of satisfaction, pride and accomplishment, or alternatively, sadness, frustration, guilt or disappointment, when reviewing visualizations of the personal data they have collected about themselves. These data can motivate them and encourage them to move their bodies more, to persist with weight-loss efforts or self-management of chronic conditions. The 'numbers' can make them feel good if they demonstrate that people are achieving goals set for themselves, or if the data demonstrate good health or higher levels of fitness. Positive feelings can be generated by the buzzes, flashing lights, badges and other notifications that communicate a goal has been achieved.

Frances, one of the participants in the Australian Women and Digital Health study, said that she regularly uses a Fitbit wearable device to monitor her physical activity. She commented that she has found herself doing things like walking around the kitchen late at night 'just to get those last steps' to make her 10,000-step daily goal. Frances said that she enjoys looking at the graphs that the app shows her on her body weight and physical activity:

> So the fact that I've got a graph showing a trend is much more satisfying to me than just having a list of things written

down in a notebook. I don't get wildly excited when it gives
me little comments like, point two of a kilo to go and this
goal is in the bag.

Frances also likes the coloured lights on the Fitbit:

> I get a pink light – the whites flash and then there's a pink
> light when I get to my 10 minutes to the hour and I haven't
> got my numbers – haven't got my 250 steps. There's a blue
> light that flashes and I get a little buzz, if I get a text message
> or a phone call on this. That is quite handy … If I actually
> get up to my 10,000 steps, you get the buzz and the flashing
> lights and all the coloured lights go. So you get a green and a
> pink and a blue. So that's pretty exciting.

Alternatively, however, personal data can have demoralizing
effects, generating disappointment, frustration, guilt and
anger. Notifications from apps or wearable devices can be
experienced as annoying or pestering, making unreasonable
demands. Amy, another participant in the Australian Women
and Digital Health study, said that she was monitoring her
diet and exercise in an attempt to lose weight. She explained
that while she usually 'feels good' in response to the details
about herself she collects, there are times when she feels
'sad and worried': if she gains weight, for example. Chloe,
a participant in the Self-Trackers study, also acknowledged
that she is not always happy with the information provided to
her via self-tracking devices. She said that she feels 'horrible'
when her apps notify her that she has spent too much or has
eaten too much, as her sense of self-control over her body
is then challenged by the app's metrics. The anticipation of
seeing 'bad' numbers can even prevent people from checking
their details. For example, Glenda, another participant in the
Self-Trackers study, discussed how she sometimes avoided
reviewing the information she had collected about herself,
describing a 'sense of shame' she sometimes felt when
confronting it.

Most of the participants in the Self-Trackers study had
voluntarily taken up monitoring of their health or fitness,
although several people with chronic illnesses had been
encouraged by their doctors to do so as part of patient
self-care regimens. It was this latter group who particularly

struggled with the burden of self-tracking demands. Ronald expressed the most negative views of all the participants in the Self-Trackers study. Ronald has diabetes, and as a result has been tracking many aspects of his health for the past five years. His doctor suggested he take up self-tracking, and he has to use a medical device for measuring his blood glucose levels as part of his self-care regimen. He also attends appointments with his doctor for regular medical monitoring and brings along his self-tracked details to report them to his doctor at these appointments.

Ronald said that he finds self-tracking to be a burden and he doesn't enjoy doing it: in his words, 'it's a pain in the bum, but I feel I have to'. Ronald went on to comment on how much work it took him both to motivate himself to engage in self-tracking and to learn how to do it successfully: 'It's something that you have to force yourself into doing. I started doing it and would forget for a few days. It's something that took me months to get into the habit of [doing].'

Ronald's frank account of how much he dislikes the intensive and time-consuming self-monitoring that is part of his self-care regimen draws attention to the hidden labour that can be part of regular self-tracking. As his descriptions demonstrate, these kinds of self-monitoring require a period of learning and adjustment so that they can be incorporated into the practices and rhythms of everyday routines. There are other negative aspects to monitoring one's body and health and illness states. It can sometimes generate information that is confronting or disappointing. Ronald said that how he feels about the information depends on what it reveals about his health. It can be both motivating and demoralizing:

> [I feel] good when I see them, when the figures are close to what I want them to be. It makes me motivated and makes me feel more controlled. It also shows me when I have to get a handle on something. If I think I did try hard and the result's not good, it makes you feel down.

As Ronald's experiences demonstrate, not only can self-monitoring chronic health problems be time-consuming and hard work, it can also be emotionally confronting. If the information generated from self-tracking practice suggests that health conditions are degenerating, weight has been gained, blood glucose levels are not well managed and so forth – even when people have done the best they can to make the numbers 'good' – the affective force of these insights can be dispiriting.

These findings suggest that there are several types of work involved in taking up and maintaining self-tracking. These include the labour of learning the techniques and incorporating them into mundane routines, the work involved in continuing to invest time and effort into these routines day after day, and the sense-making work requiring people to assess the value and accuracy of the information they are generating about themselves. People are also called upon to engage in the emotional labour required to respond to and manage the affective dimensions of regular self-tracking practices, in situations where their information can be disappointing or frustrating. These forms of labour are closely associated with the distributed agencies and capacities involved in self-tracking assemblages. The technologies used and the data they generate have certain capacities and affects as they intra-act with human bodies.

The participants' accounts provided insights into what bodies and selves are capable of when they enter into enactments of self-tracking. They also highlight how the affordances of objects like digital technologies can be recalcitrant (Bennett 2009), making demands that can be difficult for human users to meet. Identifying the frustrations, disappointments and burdens of self-tracking can demonstrate how human–technological assemblages can be generative of a range of affective forces, some of which can limit or block the capacities that people want to experience.

Data mementos

Another affective dimension of personal data is their potential to act as mementos: objects that archive and revive memories. Many devices, apps and platforms that generate, record and materialize personal data allow people the opportunity to go back and review previous materializations. In this way, personal data assemblages can be viewed as mementos, generating thing-power through the agential capacities of connecting people with their past lives and activities. Some interesting literature in cultural geography explores the enchantment and social lives of souvenirs in ways that have implications for the idea of data assemblages as mementos. Writers contributing to this work argue for the importance of paying attention to the situated, sensory and more-than-representational aspects of people's engagements with material objects such as souvenirs from their travels.

The concept of 'refracted enchantment' discussed by Nissa Ramsay (2009) draws attention to the emergent and dynamic nature of enchantment with souvenirs and its unfolding in context with other nonhumans and with humans. Ramsay notes that enchantment with souvenirs is not always achieved, and might be 'better thought of as a materialism which has "not-yet" become' (2009: 202). She argues that enchantment in relation to souvenirs can be emergent, habitual and residual. The makers and sellers of the souvenirs work to produce enchantment to attract sales, often involving claims to authenticity, uniqueness or affective or meaningful ties to the object. Once purchased, the object may generate enchantment when placed in the everyday mundane setting of the traveller's life. This enchantment may become residual if the object is routinely engaged with, and may sometimes become re-enchanted when people are reminded of the time and place in which they purchased it. Enchantment, therefore, is not fixed, but rather is highly dynamic and processual. Objects may lose and reacquire enchantment.

Similarly, Michael Haldrup (2017) takes up the concept of enchantment to portray souvenirs as magical objects in everyday life. He identifies five roles of souvenirs as enchanted objects. The first role is that of utility item: the souvenir has use value to define ourselves, inspire emotions and trigger memories. The second role is that of mediator: the souvenir forms part of networks and flows that connect people with other times, events and places. In its third role, the souvenir can tune people's bodies to affective atmospheres, or the emotional resonances that spaces can generate. The fourth role of the souvenir is that of fetish: it acts as a fragment of an experience to evoke the whole experience, both connecting people to the experiences and places of the time at which they purchased the souvenir, and representing places and times – sometimes in ways people would rather not remember because they evoke painful or discomforting memories, sensations and feelings. The fifth and final role of the souvenir is as an artwork, in which creative agency or the symbolic expression of feeling may be expressed.

Personal data materializations are often portrayed in popular media and users' accounts as possessing the forces of enchantment, with the capacity to impel human action, and as repositories of memories. Data materializations can work as souvenirs or mementos in the ways described by Ramsay and Haldrup. As I have demonstrated in this chapter, data materializations can bring people together with other humans in their lives through sharing personal details with each other, and with nonhuman things and spaces, composing strong relational connections.

Many tech entrepreneurs ascribe a certain kind of thing-power to the data materializations generated with their devices and software and their capacity to create these connections and serve as mementos. Their capacities to engage users and motivate them are often used as selling points. Strava, for example, claims that it has 'the world's best tracking' to 'track and analyse every aspect of your activity ... you can track your favourite performance stats, and afterwards, dive deep into your data'. Strava also features ways for members to provide encouragement to each other ('Connect with friends and share your adventure') and to upload images of the places they explore while running or cycling. As the Strava website puts it, 'Don't just track your adventure – show it' (Strava 2019). These promissory narratives position Strava as a tool that can generate a range of affective forces, relational connections and agential capacities: close monitoring of athletic bodies, displays of performance that can be made public to other members, the thrill and pleasure of moving through new places and spaces, opportunities to archive and display visual images of these places and spaces, the provision of support to other members, and the opportunity to compete with them for further motivation. Athletic self-monitoring, as represented by Strava, is much more than simply counting things: it is a profoundly social mode of self-identity and embodiment (Lupton 2018b).

Promotional material for another genre of monitoring software, the baby tracker app, draws on another set of promissory narratives. The blurb for the 'Baby Tracker – Newborn Log' app on the Apple App Store, for example, features cherubic photographs of smiling or sleeping infants. Potential users (described as 'busy parents') are informed that the app will help them to 'stay organized' and 'identify vital trends', by offering a 'simple, streamlined way to track your baby's daily habits, health, and exciting "firsts" of those precious early days and months'. The blurb goes on to claim that: 'Perhaps most important, Baby Tracker handles all the details so you never have to take significant time away from the joys of parenting'. Here this app is positioned as contributing to the pleasurable affective forces of parenthood – the joys and excitements – while offering a solution for the less pleasurable dimensions – worries and anxieties about a baby's development, routines and health and the challenges and demands posed by performing as a careful, responsible parent.

Both these technologies – the Strava platform and app and the Baby Tracker app – offer users the agential capacity to record personal data for posterity and to share these details with others. Not only visual images of people and places can be displayed and stored as mementos, but so too can the range of metrics that these technologies generate about their users. Where once the paper 'baby book' was used to archive photographs and details of infants' development and growth, or paper journals were used to record details of cycling trips or runs, or family photograph albums were used to archive personal images for future generations, apps or social media status updates can be used to record these data. Both analogue and digitized forms of recording can preserve experiences for posterity. They have different affordances, however. Analogue mementos can be kept more private, remaining the property of the owner or the people to whom the owner may pass on the memento. Digitized mementos are usually uploaded to and stored on proprietary databases and become the property of the developers, open to access and use by third parties. Once uploaded and transmitted to these databases, the people who have generated these personal details lose control of how their data are used and preserved.

The digital data left behind when people die can also act as mementos of the people themselves. Social media services like Facebook and Instagram and content-sharing sites like YouTube can be repositories of many intimate details about people that they have uploaded in the form of status updates, images, videos, comments and likes. Sometimes relatives or friends use these social media presences as memorials for the dead person, or create new pages specially for this purpose, posting tributes and expressions of grief and loss (Bollmer 2013; Arnold et al. 2017). Digitizing of human remains, as in photographing and videoing them with digital devices, is a way of rendering long-dead humans into digital data that can perpetrate a kind of digital immortality at the same time as it potentially renders these human remains in far more available ways to the public. These data, whether of long-dead people or those who have actively uploaded their details as part of online engagements, have been described as 'digital remains' (Stokes 2015; Ulguim 2018).

These practices raise ethical and moral issues concerning the rights of humans and what consent should be provided by people or their descendants for digitizing their bodies and other personal data. Furthermore, thorny issues around the digital memorializing of dead people using websites or social media and the use and continued storage and stewardship of people's digital data (e.g., their social media posts, profiles and uploaded images or online gaming avatars) after their death have yet to be fully confronted by platform and device developers and users (Bollmer 2013; Arnold et al. 2017). People who receive messages, reminders or notifications about or apparently from dead relatives or friends from platforms like Facebook can find this confronting and unsettling (Bassett 2018).

The generation of digital remains calls into question how human death should be understood when dead people's personal data continue to be lively and agential online. Issues are raised concerning the ownership of this information, for how long it should be stored and who should be able to delete, access or benefit from it. More profoundly, the continuing existence of these data and their digital afterlives provokes challenging consideration about their onto-ethico-epistemological status. These data are literally posthumous, continuing to possess their own vitalities, vibrancies and affective forces. Indeed, it has been contended by philosophers of information technology that deleting personal data could be considered a 'second death' for the person to whom they can be attributed, and that these data should be accorded the moral status of corpses or human body parts such as tissues or organs (Stokes 2015; Öhman and Floridi 2018).

Summary

The research discussed in this chapter highlights the dynamic nature of the more-than-human world of human–data assemblages. It points to the sensory and embodied dimensions of the ways in which humans and technologies gather and intra-act to make and do data. As performative agents, individuals are actively engaging their bodies and minds as they are 'becoming-with data' (Hultman and Lenz Taguchi 2010: 538). These are forms of lively imaginings and interpretings, in which knowing and being cannot be separated (Barad 2003). Human–data assemblages can generate agential capacities that shape people's embodied responses and actions, their sense of selfhood and their relationships with other people and with other things. These reflections make a contribution to understanding how personal data come to matter in people's lives and acknowledging the work involved in making sense of data selves.

5

Sharing and Exploiting Data

Personal data practices can potentially include sharing details with others in ways that can help to develop and promote social networks and relationships and to accumulate a communal body of knowledge. However, these details can reveal patterns in people's lives and bodily experiences that they may not wish others to know about, much less profit from. This chapter discusses the tension that therefore exists between the sharing ethos of digital media – particularly online discussion forums and social media platforms – and concerns about the privacy of personal data. As I show, an approach to personal data sharing and privacy drawing on feminist new materialism can contribute to and extend current theorizing about online privacy in further emphasizing the connectedness, relationality and affective dimensions of these agencies.

Participatory sharing and intimate surveillance

The ethos of participatory sharing underpins the ways in which people choose to disclose information about themselves to others online. The dominant norms of sharing on social media often expect reciprocity of information sharing and self-disclosure. Social media users are encouraged to share, 'like' or comment on other members' content (Gerlitz and Helmond 2013; van Dijck 2013). Many of the pleasures and benefits that internet users gain from engaging online involve uploading details about themselves for the review of other users, inviting their responses and responding to others in turn (Albrechtslund and Lauritsen 2013; John 2017). Digital media can provide a space in which people can exchange personal details, thoughts and feelings, become friends and develop feelings of intimacy: in some cases, without ever meeting face to face (Kuntsman 2012; Chambers 2013; Lambert 2013).

Self-trackers are encouraged to share their data in some forums. For example, the 'show-and-tell' mode of performing self-tracking and publicly revealing personal details is a standard practice for members of the Quantified Self community. This practice involves attending meetings of members or the annual Quantified Self conferences and delivering a presentation that focuses on how the presenters practise self-tracking and detailing the insights they have gained from it. Some of these show-and-tells are video-recorded and uploaded to the official Quantified Self website and thus made available to any internet user (Lupton 2016b). Online patient support groups encourage members to share their health and medical details as a way of contributing to peer networks of expertise and support (Ziebland and Wyke 2012; Lupton 2014). Internet forums for people monitoring their physical activity or weight loss efforts can also allow people to engage in confessional genres of sharing, where they reveal 'bad' data and seek redemption and moral support from other users (Niva 2017; Esmonde and Jette 2018). Keen athletes who use 'social fitness' platforms such as Strava (Lupton 2018b) often appreciate the support, competition and feelings of achievement and prowess that they experience with uploading their physical activity details to the platforms for other members to view and comment on (Stragier et al. 2015; Lupton et al. 2018), thereby developing communities of practice (Smith and Treem 2017). In these contexts, the sharing of personal experiences online becomes a communal data practice, in which people's personal details become part of a crowdsourced body of knowledge that is available to other users of the sites.

In my research studies, these kinds of social interactions were an important part of some participants' use of digital self-monitoring technologies or online discussion forums. In the Self-Tracking Cyclists project, while not all the participants chose to share their cycling data with others, for several this feature was integral to how they used platforms like Strava and interpreted their data. The possibilities offered by self-tracking and the potential for sharing this information in a public space/platform and comparing one's data with other users could be experienced emotionally in several different ways, the affective forces and agential capacities generated by these practices shaping people's decisions about how long to track for and what to do with their data.

For example, Neil, who monitored his cycle trips and his running and swimming activities (he is training for triathlon competitions), said that he can hardly wait to arrive home before rushing to download his data and compare the details with other users:

> The first thing I do is download that data and see if I've got any course records or things like that. I'm kind of obsessed with going for local course records or testing myself on certain courses.

Rebecca also made repeated reference to the affective dimensions of self-tracking her cycling and making use of Strava. She noted that she sometimes tracked her rides for competitive reasons and found this 'an enjoyable aspect of training', helping her continue with her arduous regimen. Rebecca explained that in the first couple of years using Strava, her use of the platform for self-tracking her cycling trips made her ride faster, and more competitively. She now 'doesn't care so much', but she sometimes sets herself weekly distance goals, particularly when she is training for a forthcoming event.

The term 'intimate surveillance' has been adopted to describe the mode of watching that takes place when people observe other people who are close to them, such as friends, spouses, sexual or romantic partners, children and other family members (Levy 2015; Leaver 2017). Many forms of intimate surveillance undertaken online using discussion forums or social media groups are undertaken as means of establishing and maintaining social relationships and engendering mutual feelings of closeness via shared knowledge. People who may feel socially isolated can benefit from engaging in these groups with other people in their situation, finding opportunities to share experiences, find friendship and relieve loneliness. Very personal details about people's states of health and wellbeing or their moods and feelings can be expressed and shared in these forums. Some forms of intimate surveillance are intertwined with caring practices, such as the monitoring that parents may undertake of their children's health, wellbeing and development.

In my research projects involving interviews and focus groups with women who were pregnant or caring for infants (the Australian Women's Use of Digital Media for Pregnancy and Parenting and the Australian Women and Digital Health projects), this kind of sharing of personal details was very common. Women identified apps, online forums and social media groups that they found valuable to support their wellbeing and their experiences of motherhood. The women particularly appreciated the intimacy of the relational connections they were able to build by using these digital media. They used pregnancy tracking apps to monitor the progress of their pregnancies and to learn about how their bodies were changing and their foetus was developing week by week. For example, one woman described why she liked using one particular pregnancy app:

> It is really cool, so you can actually go, week 29 and have a look and see what your baby's doing and it'll give you like a rundown of what's happening in there. And then it also gives you a section on what's happening in your body, so what hormones are causing what. And then it gives you a rundown of symptoms that you might be having for that week, so it might be heartburn. [It has] Everything!

Once their babies were born, another raft of apps was used to track their development, growth, feeding and sleeping patterns and achievement of milestones. These details could be shared with their partners and friends and family members by uploading them to Facebook. Sharing images of their children online was a regular practice described by these women. Facebook was commonly used for this purpose, but some women also used Instagram, uploading photographs of their children to share with followers, or the Tiny Beans app, which could be used to share baby photos with selected recipients via email notifications. Several women also followed other people's Instagram or Pinterest accounts, mainly to view children's clothing styles or other commodity-related content.

The immediacy of peer information and support that was available online was also highly valued by the participants. The participants in the focus groups spoke about the importance of being able to exchange details of their experiences with other mothers and seek their advice if needed. Online discussion forums and Facebook groups allowed women to seek reassurance from women who had experienced similar events or problems. As two women in a focus group said of the information they accessed online when they were pregnant:

> Participant: It puts your mind at ease, and you want to know that you're normal, and everything's normal, and you're going to have a normal pregnancy, you know.
> Participant: Like the online forums are good, because it's nice, even though like a midwife, someone might say to you, 'Oh, everyone gets a bit depressed during pregnancy,' or whatever, there's actual evidence of people saying 'I felt like this, I felt like that.'

Several stories were recounted by the women of feeling anxious or worried in the middle of the night with a tiny baby to care for who may not be sleeping or feeding well, or was ill. In this situation, being able to go online and find forums, on which other mothers describe dealing with the same issues, was very helpful. Most participants also noted that access to online information helped them when they were feeling isolated, with no one else to turn to for advice and support. Sometimes women want to discuss a topic that they consider private or sensitive and therefore perhaps not easy to raise with family members or healthcare professionals. Online forums that provide anonymity and the opportunity to discuss these kinds of issues with other mothers were particularly valued for these uses. A participant used the example of sexual activity during pregnancy:

> I think another issue is sex – having sex since the first time when you know you're pregnant, and all that kind of stuff, which is stuff that you might not want to talk to your mum about. And it's good, really honest responses.

This exchange of information was a way of establishing and developing social relationships. Some participants noted that they felt emotionally close to the women they had come to know on forums or social media because of these shared exchanges. While information offered by professionals was highly valued when women had a specific health-related concern, the intimacy provided by the emotional support and connection offered by other mothers online was an important factor for many women. The types of information exchanged on platforms used by the women in this research were valued not only for the advice that they offer but also because they are part of the currency of friendships and social networks.

These digitized practices of participatory sharing and intimate surveillance generated a range of affective forces and agential capacities. They helped women feel better connected not only to their peers but also to their foetuses and children. Using pregnancy-tracking apps or infant-monitoring apps, for example, was a way for women to develop a relationship with their foetuses or children and to feel that the women understood them better, as well as providing reassurance that their foetuses and children were developing and growing as they should. Being able to distribute images of their children online was another way for women to share their feelings of love, excitement and pride in their children with friends and family.

Sharing personal details about oneself or one's children can also support social relationships that operate face to face. In my Australian Self-Trackers project, the participants were mostly tracking health-related, physical activity, diet and financial details. Most of the participants used digital technologies such as apps or spreadsheets for recording their self-tracking details, although several also used pen and paper or maintained mental awareness and memories of their details. However, very few people said that they shared the details they collected about themselves with others online, or that they were engaging in self-tracking communities of any kind. Despite the high level of media and academic research attention given to the Quantified Self community, none of the participants made any mention of the term 'quantified self', the Quantified Self website or community, or attending any group meetings related to self-tracking such as those run by the Quantified Self community and similar self-tracking groups. They were not participating in workplace challenges or other initiatives that attempt to 'nudge' people into communal forms of self-tracking (Lupton 2016a). These participants' self-tracking was conducted for the most part as a solitary activity, and for most of them it did not involve comparing their data with others who were engaging in similar self-tracking activities, either for competitive or support purposes.

The notion that these details should be kept private from online forums underpinned much of these participants' reluctance to tell others about the information they had collected about themselves. The personal and often sensitive nature of these details and the belief that other people would not be interested in them were key concerns in the participants' accounts. Nick, for example, said that he rarely shares his data with anyone, whether in online forums or in face-to-face encounters.

> I rarely – virtually never – share my details online. Finances are a private matter. Health and nutrition – I just don't really want to bore my friends with it. Occasionally I have, but it's not very common.

Some participants expressed a negative stance about the idea of sharing their self-tracked details on social media platforms in particular. Glenda said that she disapproved of the ways in which some people 'pour their hearts out' on social media and noted that she had seen 'some very negative behaviour and relationships breaking down, and some very negative conversations on social media'. In contrast, she said, 'I guess I'm quite private with what I share.' Glenda reported that she discusses some of the financial details she tracks with her husband, as well as some emotional information, as both types of details are relevant to their relationship.

Like Glenda, several other people noted that they occasionally talked about their self-tracked details with their partners or other family members or close friends. This sharing was sometimes conducted to demonstrate 'what works' for achieving such goals as weight loss or saving money. For example, Kerry commented that she likes to share details with her friends about things she has learnt from tracking her expenditure sometimes: when talking about how to reduce energy bills. For Maria, talking with her friends and family about what she has learnt about managing her finances, weight loss or her daughter's asthma condition is a way of helping them learn about the best ways to approach similar goals:

> So that it can help them whenever they choose to lose a bit of weight or something. Or so that they learn how to manage their finances or handle their asthma problems, or whatever.

These participants presented the practice of discussing details of what they have learnt about themselves with others as a way of contributing to the everyday communicative interactions that are part of their social relationships. Pamela said that she talks about her health a lot with co-workers and family members face to face, and she enjoys this aspect of sharing. In her case, it is a reciprocal relationship. She shares the insights she has gained from self-tracking with her co-workers and in turn learns from them. Pamela works in what she describes as a 'stressful industry', and she finds that this exchange of personal details is a way of contributing to other people's wellbeing at work as well as her own.

For Carol, another person who engaged in regular self-tracking, it was important to let her close friends and family know about her health-related self-tracked information, as they cared about her and she felt that they would want to be informed. Carol viewed this reciprocal sharing as part of mutually supportive relationships, as she also wanted to stay informed of their medical details.

I'm on Facebook, but I don't really share anything like that on Facebook. I probably tell family members about my health or a very close friend, yes. Just to see if they've had similar experiences and if they can recommend something as well. I've got a friend who's got chronic back pain, so I would ring up another friend or just go by my own experience, I would probably mention it.

Howard's view on the importance of sharing self-tracked details with intimate others insightfully sums up most people's attitudes.

I occasionally share my details, yes. Not online, but face to face. Family members and friends. I think it's because there's a value in sharing stuff with people rather than not, if you know what I mean. Somehow, it's like if you share that secret, it's a part of bringing people into your personal life. Sharing leads to caring in that way, I guess.

These comments point to the idea that talking about self-tracked details with friends and family members can be viewed as an act of altruism, demonstrating caring and interest in other people. Here again, the participatory sharing ethos and practices of intimate surveillance converge with various forms of self-monitoring and the monitoring of apps using both digital technologies and other types of encounters with close others in people's lives. For some people, sharing details about themselves or their family members on digital media is integral to finding the relational connections with other people that they need. For others, using digitized information in face-to-face encounters serves this purpose of strengthening intimate relationships.

Reconceptualizing personal data privacy

As outlined in chapter 1, the ethos of participatory sharing on social media has now become harnessed to commercial and neoliberal rationales. The 'archives of affect' (Gehl 2011) that digital companies have amassed and can exploit are the product of the unpaid labour of users of social media. In surveillance capitalism (Zuboff 2015), the personal details generated by online interactions and mobile device use are exploited by a diverse range of third parties, both legally and illicitly. These data have become open to repurposing for commercial, research, governmental, managerial, security and criminal actors and agencies as part of the global digital knowledge economy. The use of people's personal details extends well beyond any original intention that they may have had in gathering them. The intimate relational connections they have chosen to establish with other people online are part of much larger networks of data sharing that are often mysterious or hidden to users.

In response to these controversies and risks related to personal data, some individuals and organizations have begun to call for citizens to develop data privacy literacy and skills in data privacy self-management (Obar 2015). Kennedy and Moss (2015) argue that a move from 'known' to 'knowing' (reflexive and active) publics needs to occur as part of enhancing citizens' agency over their personal data. Other researchers have called for people's access to their own data to be enhanced, so that data divides or information asymmetries between internet corporations, large organizations and governments, on the one hand, and publics, on the other, are less stark (Andrejevic 2014; Mittelstadt and Floridi 2016).

As I noted in chapter 3, many commentators in the mass media have begun to draw attention to publics' alleged sense of lack of agency and loss of control in relation to their digitized information. Some news reports have suggested that publics have little or no interest in preserving, managing or exerting control over their personal data privacy. Moral censure and victim-blaming of publics can occur in media reporting of data breaches and leaks, particularly if the online interactions involved are considered morally dubious. The millions of people worldwide affected by the hacking of the adultery dating site Ashley Madison in 2015 were often depicted in news reports as deserving their loss of privacy and any related moral censure or relationship breakdown because of their willing participation in meeting others online outside their marriages. When the Cambridge Analytica/Facebook scandal erupted in the news media in 2018, it was suggested in some reports that internet users had only themselves to blame for allowing their personal data to be open to questionable third-party use, due to laziness or ignorance. One example is the news story published in the *Guardian* by Dylan Curran (2018), in which he accessed his personal data held by Facebook and Google to demonstrate how voluminous their records about him were. Curran asserted that:

> This information has millions of nefarious uses ... This is one of the craziest things about the modern age. We would never let the government or a corporation put camera/microphones in our homes or location trackers on us. But we just went ahead and did it ourselves because – to hell with it! – I want to watch cute dog videos. (Curran 2018)

News coverage has begun to suggest that the frequency of these types of personal data scandals over the past half-decade or so has led to members of the public feeling powerless, fatalistic or complacent. An article in the *New York Times*, for example, headlined 'Data breaches keep happening. So why don't you do something?' claimed 'experts worry that people are just throwing up their hands in defeat' and are experiencing 'breach fatigue' (Mele 2018).

Over a decade ago, and before the ascendancy of Facebook and self-tracking apps, at its most extreme, the question 'In the age of digital media, do we really have any privacy?' was asked (Barnes 2006). The term 'privacy paradox' has been employed to describe the apparent contradiction between publics articulating concern about their personal data privacy but also freely contributing intimate details about their lives to online forums such as social media (Barnes 2006; Kokolakis 2017). These days, internet and legal scholars provide a more nuanced stance. They argue that new digital technologies have had a profound effect on concepts and practices of privacy that remain in flux as changes occur in the ways in which personal information is collected, stored and used. The current complicated scenario of dynamic data generation, collection, sharing and exploitation calls into question traditional modes of understanding and regulating information privacy (Leszczynski 2015). The privacy paradox has been problematized by researchers seeking to surface the complexities of public understandings of personal data privacy. According to Jonathan Obar (2015), for example, data privacy self-management is a fallacy perpetuated by governments that ignores the complexity of the infrastructural affordances in which personal data are generated, archived and repurposed by secondary users.

Instead of the traditional Westernized theory of autonomous privacy, which represents it as related to the rights of individualized selfhood (Bannerman 2018), many privacy scholars now frequently argue for a 'networked privacy' concept, which acknowledges that sharing of personal details online often inadvertently involves revealing other people's details. Privacy in relation to online data therefore cannot be understood as the right or privilege of an individual (Marwick and boyd 2014). Another concept that has been offered in response to new digital media communication is that of 'relational privacy' (Bannerman 2018). Both the networked privacy and relational privacy concepts critique the idea of autonomous privacy, highlighting the distributed nature of privacy as it is performed in digital media. The concept of 'contextual privacy' acknowledges that the relational, spatial and temporary aspects of personal data sharing shape privacy concepts (Nissenbaum 2011). A further distinction has been drawn between 'social privacy' and 'institutional privacy' in terms of how social media users understand privacy. Social privacy refers to the extent to which known intimate others, such as friends and family, are able to access and view personal information uploaded online. Institutional privacy concerns how institutions such as corporations and government agencies access this kind of information (Raynes-Goldie 2010).

Publics' responses

Several studies in different countries in the Global North have shown most people are well aware that their personal information is collected by the internet empires, other corporations and governments, but are unsure about the details of exactly who is conducting dataveillance on them and how their data are being shared with third parties. Kennedy and colleagues

(2017) undertook focus groups in the UK, Norway and Spain about attitudes to social media data mining. They found that there was an approximately equal number of people who found personalized targeted advertising on Facebook concerning compared with those who were not worried by it. However, participants were far more concerned about their Facebook data being shared with third parties, and about employers monitoring employees' comments about their company on social media sites. Issues of consent were important to the participants: many felt negatively about users' social media being accessed without their knowledge or consent, or being combined for profiling purposes in ways of which they were unaware. This research also highlighted the issue that participating on social media platforms often feels private and intimate, because it can involve contributions about very personal issues, and therefore it can be difficult to acknowledge that these contributions can be treated as public information by the platform owners, data mining companies or researchers.

For the young adults in the United States who took part in focus groups to discuss internet privacy issues (Hargittai and Marwick 2016), an understanding of privacy threats was coupled with the resignation that they could not do much to protect their personal data. They were well aware of the risks of sharing personal information online, as they had experienced incidents of embarrassing or revealing details being exposed or knew someone who had experienced this. These participants tended to focus on these kinds of social risks rather than potential harms from secondary exploitation of their data. Beyond the commercial use of their details by third parties, most of the participants were unsure which other actors might be accessing and exploiting their data. They knew that Facebook posts, for example, were public and could be shared by other Facebook users, but felt that they could do little to prevent this sharing from occurring or to stop hackers and cybercriminals accessing the personal data. The only effective measure they felt they could take was not to upload personal details to social media platforms in the first place.

Research with young people living in London similarly found that most participants reported taking steps to protect their privacy by not revealing personal details such as relationship status and personal thoughts and feelings on social media sites (Sujon 2018). These participants made a distinction between these kinds of details (considered 'private') and other information about themselves that they did not consider to be 'private' and therefore did not need to be protected (such as their name, age and purchasing history). Personal data privacy was understood to be something that they could control in terms of the decisions they made about what personal information they chose to upload to social media sites.

These beliefs and behaviours are not limited to young people. A Canadian study involving people aged 65 years and over elicited similar findings. Both users of social media and non-users in this group were concerned about protecting their personal information from unauthorized access and misuse; this is one reason people had chosen not to use social media. Those people who did use social media attempted not to share information they wanted to protect on these platforms (Quan-Haase and Elueze 2018). A survey on digital rights in Australia across a range of age groups, supplemented with a small number of focus groups (Goggin et al. 2017), found that the respondents were most concerned about corporations violating their privacy, followed by government and other people. A large majority wanted to know what social media companies did with their personal data. Although most respondents did not feel in control of their privacy online, a large proportion had taken steps to protect their privacy, such as changing settings on social media. In their focus group study involving Britons, Hintz and colleagues (2019) found that their participants often mentioned engaging in similar activities relating to their social media use, but were far less likely to report using private browsers or mail encryption technologies because they either lacked the knowledge to do so or wanted to avoid inconvenience.

Focus groups with British publics similarly found that while people were highly aware of being watched using dataveillance, they were uncertain about how and why their personal information was being collected (Hintz et al. 2019). A survey of Canadian university students' understandings of digital geolocation data collection (Leszczynski 2015) found that participants were more concerned with transparency in data collection and in controlling flows of their personal spatial data at their source than with the eventual secondary use of the data. The 'data anxieties' that the participants evinced concerning how their spatial data entered into circulation in the digital data economy recognized that this is the point at which they can lose control over their data, and therefore the only time at which they can potentially limit how much of their spatial data are generated and who is able to have access to these details.

As these findings suggest, there are limitations to what people can do on their own behalf to protect their personal data. There are some steps that people can take to protect their data privacy and security. They can attempt to read terms and conditions and privacy policies of apps and other software (if they are provided and if they are written in user-friendly terminology), limit how many apps and platforms they use, check their privacy settings, avoid using public WiFi networks, switch from mainstream search engines and browsers to more private ones and so on. However, apart from events that receive high levels of news coverage, publics are often not informed, or have no way of knowing, when their personal data are breached, hacked or stolen, or used in other ways that may harm them. When moving around in public spaces, they may not be aware of how sensors are documenting their movements or using facial recognition software to identify them.

Added to these complexities are the difficulties that many internet and mobile technology users face in understanding or accessing the terms and conditions of the software and hardware that they use, which are often written in dense and lengthy prose (Rosenzweig 2012; Tene and Polonetsky 2013b). Sometimes people agree to the use of their personal data as an unavoidable part of accepting the terms and conditions of devices, apps and platforms (although to what extent users actually read through the fine print on these documents is not known) or signing up to customer loyalty schemes. In other cases, their data may be accessed for the purposes of others without their knowledge or consent. Developers often fail to inform users that their data are available to third parties (Sarasohn-Kahn 2014). Platform and apps developers can change their privacy policies without warning, often without the knowledge of users (Hargittai and Marwick 2016).

More broadly, a major barrier to people being able to fully identify and understand what happens to their personal data is the vast and constantly changing networks of data sharing that exchange people's data and the lack of control they are able to exert once the data are transmitted to cloud computing archives. This was evident in a project Mike Michael and I undertook with people living in Sydney using cultural probes to inspire discussion of how everyday citizens were monitored by data-generating technologies (Lupton and Michael 2017). The study uncovered the prevailing dominance in public understandings of data of tacit assumptions about the uses and benefits of dataveillance as well as fears and anxieties about its possible misuse. Our research participants were able to identify a range of ways in which dataveillance is conducted, but were more aware of obvious commercial and some government actors. There was very little identification of the types of dataveillance that are used by national security and policing agencies or of illegal access by hackers and cybercriminals.

Across several other research projects I have conducted involving Australians discussing their use of digital technologies and digital data, I have included questions that have asked participants if they ever think about what happens to their personal data, and if they have any concerns about how third parties might be accessing and using their details. Regardless of the group or topic under discussion, few participants have expressed major concerns about their personal data privacy and security. Importantly, while participants often valued highly the agential capacity of digital technologies to generate detailed information about their bodies and health states, for the most part they did not recognize the capacities these very personal data offered to other actors and agencies. On the contrary, the most commonly imagined affordance of the idea of digital health technology was a website or app which could collect even more detailed information about the user and bring these data together all in one place. This imagined device was valued for convenience, ease of use and the detailed information it could generate and curate.

The potential for these data to be used or exploited by third parties was not considered to be important by many participants. They seemed to lack either knowledge or care about where their personal information went and who used it. For example, few of the participants in the Australian Self-Trackers study who used digital technologies for self-tracking had given much thought to the privacy and security of their personal data generated from self-tracking, even their financial details. The potential porosity of cloud computing and the possibilities of data leakages, breaches or hacking did not seem to have occurred to them. Margaret, who uses a blood pressure monitor and blood sugar monitor, said she thought it unlikely that anyone else would be interested in her health information. Sarah acknowledged that the information she records about herself is 'obviously personal, but it's not something that I feel like could be used to steal my identity or identity fraud anything like that. It can't be used in any malicious way'.

Some people said that they had considered the risks to some extent, but were still not very concerned. Paul contended:

> I've got [my information] fairly locked away within the apps, or the devices I've got or on the computer. So I don't really have a concern about it. It's always possible that things can get leaked, but I'm pretty happy and feel safe with the stuff I've got.

Chloe did note that she was aware that there may be some risk to the security of her financial information stored in her PocketBook app, but this did not worry her enough to relinquish its use:

> Pocket Book's got all my bloody banking information. So yes, definitely I think about data security. Do I consider it when I sign up? No. Do I worry? No. But I understand that the risk is there and it could happen.

The findings of my 'Data Personas' project illustrated some of the understandings and imaginaries underpinning this apparent lack of concern about personal data privacy. Using the cultural probe of the 'data persona' was a way of inviting people to think about these issues imaginatively. A definition of the data persona was provided to the participants as follows:

> A version of you made by finding personal information about you from when you move around in spaces embedded with sensors or use digital devices like smartphones, wearable technologies, tablet computers, laptops and desktop computers.

The participants were asked to consider how their data persona might be configured and used by themselves and others. Their responses demonstrated that for the most part, people were highly aware of the many different kinds of personal information that were recorded in response to their online interactions. According to the participants, the details that potentially could be used to create their data personas included their name, date of birth, where they live, partner/family details, profession and place of work, physical appearance, browsing history, shopping habits, transport movements, topics that are followed or liked online, references (likes/dislikes) and interests. It was these details that contributed to the similarities the participants thought their data persona would have.

Nearly all the participants suggested that their data persona would be an accurate representation of themselves in some ways. However, most people argued that there would be many dimensions of themselves and their life experiences that would not be encapsulated in their data persona. The following accounts of Peter and Jo exemplify this response.

> My data persona would be very similar, know my haunts and activities, my travels, my habits, drinking, smoking and more. It would know where I shop, how I travel, maybe even my state of health. It would probably know my height and weight, my skin, hair and eye colour. It would mimic my choices and preferences. It would hold my views and persuasions, political leaning, prejudices, likes and dislikes. It would be very similar at a point in time, a snapshot, but would not comprehend my thinking and reasons for my positions. It would not understand my reasoning, thought processes

and underlying history of my life and the directions I have travelled. (Peter)

I think the data would give a good indication of the real me – it would show where I go, who my friends are, what I'm interested in, where I shop, how much I earn, where I live, where I travel to and how often, who my children and partner are, my demographic, my family profile, the music I like, the TV shows I like. I think this persona would behave like me, although I think as we all tend to put the best version of ourselves out there, there wouldn't be a lot of information about my more negative emotions and mental health issues that wouldn't be readily available ... Data profilers can know a lot about you but not your feelings about things (unless you put those about everything on Facebook, which some people do!). They cannot know what your family relationships are like, what your everyday emotions are like. They can know what your qualifications are but not necessarily your skills in some areas (i.e. whether you are good at what you do). (Jo)

Later in the discussions, participants were asked to detail how data profilers might configure their data persona and what details about themselves data profilers could never access. As is evident in these responses and across the participants' accounts, the details they thought data profilers cannot access or know about them included their emotions, mood and feelings, thoughts, secrets, bodily sensations and sensory responses, spirituality, moral beliefs, personality, irrationalities, hopes, dreams and aspirations. As Jack put it:

I used to think they wouldn't have access to emotional details; however, social media has become a platform in which we express our true feelings without fear. I still think they don't have access to one's spiritual or even heritage-based information. These are feelings that remain deep within a person, are private and not often shared. Any dark secrets or history.

These aspects were considered to be the most private, ineffable, non-measurable, embodied 'human' aspects of a person: what predominantly distinguished them from others. Participants also singled out such features that they considered to be important details about themselves as their personal biography and experiences, their historical and all their current family relationships and connections (the 'family tree', as Donna put it). Several people commented that offline conversations and practices would not be accessed by dataveillance ('because I don't do everything online', said Kieran). These are features of individuals that were considered closed off and protected from others' gaze.

The performative nature of selfhood as it is expressed online (and particularly on social media) was referred to in several participants' accounts. As Jo suggested, 'we all tend to put the best version of ourselves out there', and therefore the self that they performed on social media sites like Facebook tended to be the positive presentation of a person and their lives, rather than negative thoughts and feelings. Justin put it this way:

> The data persona would represent more so my digital self, not my entire self. It would be different to the real me based on my actions – how I act in person and on the computer are different personalities. For example, in real life I would tell people I'm very quiet, nice person etc. but online I may express certain ideals (religion, culture, likes/dislikes) in a different way to portray myself in a different way. This would in turn change the way certain information is collected about me, making it not 100% accurate, as it would be very hard to detect truth, emotion, sarcasm, etc., on what I would be saying online rather than if I would be saying it face to face.

As Jo's and Justin's words suggest, some people maintain a distinction between the 'online self' and the 'offline self', and view the 'offline self' as more authentic and real, because it is less performative. Justin also makes another point: the difficulty data profilers would have in trying to accurately assess the tone of his contributions to social media. Justin's account points to the importance of knowing the context in which such content is uploaded and the more nuanced and sophisticated cues that are offered in face-to-face communication compared with online interactions.

These findings go some way towards casting some light on the apparent 'privacy paradox'. While many participants acknowledged the existence of a distributed body/self, as represented in the figure of the data persona, they were reluctant to relinquish the idea of the inherent, closed-off, non-mediated body/self that they believed resided in the non-datafied spaces of their lives, and particularly inside their individuated bodies. They felt that key elements of themselves, such as their most private thoughts and feelings, were not (yet) accessed or documented in digital media and digital data assemblages.

Summary

The findings of my research projects and other researchers' studies discussed in this chapter suggest that it is the very liveliness, intimacy and multiple relationality of human–data assemblages that pose the greatest challenge to protecting personal data privacy. The agential capacities that people can mobilize in response to these issues are limited by the affordances of the technologies that collect and distribute personal data and the demands and constraints of the digital data and dataveillance economies. It is only when apparently immaterial data begin to have material effects/affects that they can readily be encountered and understood. Data anxieties of control tend to be focused at the level of devices, digital services and applications, as these are the technologies with which users have direct contact and of which they have the most knowledge. People are engaging in embodied and sensory ways with these devices and interfaces and can at least partially discern how their data are generated and materialized. In contrast, the movements of their personal data from the device and platform into the broader digital data economy cannot readily be discerned using embodied affordances. These data circulations are far more abstract and apparently immaterial. It is difficult to imagine one's everyday, mundane activities, such as searching the internet, using apps, making texts and calls on one's smartphone and simply just carrying the phone around, as an avenue to losing control of one's personal information. The notion that actors unknown might be spying on one's activities that are part of day-to-day life is hard to reconcile with the sheer taken-for-granted and intimate nature of these activities.

Final Thoughts

In this book, I have developed a perspective on personal digital data that proposes new metaphors and concepts beyond the archetypal. I have sought to show that data selves are more-than-personal because they are always more-than-individual and more-than-human. I have contended that personal data, like other forms of mediated representations of bodies and selves, are lively, dynamic assemblages of humans and nonhumans that are constantly subject to change. Personal data assemblages relate not only to humans' activities, feelings and movements and their associations and relationships with other people, but also to people's encounters and intra-actions with other nonhuman actors. I have argued that from the feminist new materialism perspective, personal data and humans are viewed as always part of each other, and emerge together. Just as it can be claimed that authors and books write each other (Barad 2007: x), it can also be asserted that people and their data make each other.

The perspectives and concepts I have taken up from feminist new materialism theory emphasize the vital forces and agencies that can be generated and distributed when humans assemble with technological nonhumans. This is a new conceptualization that moves well on from ideas of 'data literacy' that tend to be espoused in literatures on information sense-making. In broader terms, bringing organic and animist metaphors and concepts into the discourse on personal data works towards a greater emphasis on the inextricable aspects of more-than-human worlds, and novel ways in which digital technologies and the data they generate are part of human embodiment and selfhood. Humans are more-than-data just as personal data are more-than-human. Living with data is a mode of being, making and becoming. These data are not inscribed on bodies: they work with and through bodies.

In this book, I have attempted to focus not only on what humans can do with their data and how they can learn from their data, but how data make them feel, move and respond as part of the more-than-human worlds of which data selves are part. The *sine qua non* of digital devices and software designed for generating personalized data about humans is making the information they produce intelligible to the users: making this information known to people at the same time as they generate knowledge about people. I have argued that conventional ways of thinking about how humans 'do' data may be productively expanded by acknowledging the thing-power of digital data assemblages and directing attention to the processes of making, knowing, transforming, composing, decomposing, recomposing, articulating and incorporating that the work of data sense demands.

Building on this perspective, I have sought to consider the onto-ethico-epistemological considerations of personal data by thinking with feminist new materialism. An affirmative ethical analysis can consider the relational connections, affective forces and agential capacities that are generated when humans come together with digital devices designed to generate, store, manipulate and materialize details about them. Features of technological design (their affordances) are entangled with the enfleshed affordances of human bodies (such as bodies' capacities to be aware of and move through their surroundings, to sense, feel, manipulate and remember). Relational connections can be established between humans and other humans, but also between humans and nonhumans, generating affective forces. All of these elements may gather to configure agential capacities, or in some cases, to close these capacities off.

Feminist new materialism takes up the question of how an ethical approach to analysis can be enacted in relation to the vitalities of matter such as human–data assemblages. By adopting an affirmative ethics, I am working towards an 'ethics of care' (de la Bellacasa 2012) that can perhaps contribute to a new way of conceptualizing personal data by re-humanizing them: showing how they make humans and make a difference in people's lives in ways that can be productive but also limiting. The notion, from Barad, of identifying matter and how it comes to matter, directs us to think about digital data as a form of matter and to focus attention on the ways in which they affect human lives. Identifying the complex ways in which these affordances operate, and whose interests they serve, can begin to get to the heart of the moral, political and ethical implications concerning data selves. What ethical relations should we have with our data assemblages? What should our responsibilities be to and with them? What kinds of agential capacities are opened up or closed off?

Digital data assemblages and their algorithmic manipulation work to enact difference across a range of times and spaces. One way in which data matter is to configure people's experiences of identity and embodiment when they come together with their data. As part of automated decision-making regimes, data are exploited to distinguish between individuals and social groups. When actors engage in generating and using personal data, they are enacting agential cuts. Digital devices and software offer affordances that work to distinguish between what kinds of attributes about human lives and bodies are singled out as open to or worthy of digitizing and how this documentation and materialization should occur. These affordances are themselves enacted by human–technological assemblages: human fleshly and sensory affordances and capacities gathering with technological affordances and capacities. Along with relational connections and affective forces, affordances work to enact the responsibility of human–data assemblages in the way conceptualized by Barad. Certain human–data assemblages are more or less responsive, depending on the contexts in which they come together.

For the participants in my studies, their data mattered in many ways. Personal data were represented, above all, as forceful, generative and often enchanting. The participants referred time and again to the relational connections between themselves and their data assemblages, and the affective forces that were generated in and through their enactments of self-tracking. Their data were characterized as motivating, encouraging, building confidence, attesting to people developing better control over their lives and contributing to their social relationships – but also sometimes as discouraging, annoying or disappointing. Some of the participants also drew attention to the relational connections they sought to make between different forms of data they collected about themselves, in the attempt to discern relationships and patterns.

The affordances of digital or analogue recording of details and of data materializations (digitized graphs or numbers, written information on paper) worked to render aspects such as bodily sensations or financial expenditure visible and knowable. For many participants, their personal data were viewed as telling the truth about their lives and activities in ways that the fleshly affordances of their bodies (their sensory perceptions, their faulty memories) could not. Personal data were not necessarily accepted unproblematically, however. It was apparent in the ways in which the participants discussed their intra-actions with their data that generating these details, making sense of them and incorporating this information into their lives involved acts of emotional, mental and embodied labour. Data did not simply 'speak' for people's bodies and lives. They required the routinized work of generation and interpretation as people gathered with their data. When people were happy to rely on their bodies' affordances for monitoring themselves, it was their own capacities to continue to exert awareness and commit details to memory that supported their data enactments.

At another level of ethical inquiry, we should ask whose interests are served or neglected when agential cuts are made in response to digital datasets? These questions move from the micro-political to the macro-political level of analysis by incorporating a focus on how different social groups are defined, made visible and then acted on by other actors and agencies when their personal data are generated and manipulated through the affordances of digitized dataveillance. The selection of some attributions of people or social groups over others for configuring their data selves and the ways in which these data are materialized involve relations of power which work to make these data matter more than other details. Further inquiries into human–data assemblages require a sustained focus on these differential enactments of mattering. As I have shown in this book, many dystopian imaginaries of how well internet and data-profiling companies 'know you' currently circulate in the popular media. Too much knowledge about people is portrayed as repressive of their autonomy in these representations. What these imaginaries tend to abnegate is the many mistakes and inaccuracies that data-profiling or harvesting companies make when analysing big data and making inferences and predictions about people. In fact, it could be contended that the more serious problem for people's data rights and autonomies is not so much how detailed is these companies' or government agencies' knowledge of citizens, but the inaccuracies or absences in the data they hold on people. With the increasing move towards governments using digital data to make policy decisions or algorithmic decision-making systems responding to people's information to make recommendations or special offers, data 'invisibility' can intensify socio-economic disadvantage, as the needs of people or social groups who are not incorporated into data-profiling activities remain unrecognized. In these contexts, the internet 'not knowing enough' rather than 'knowing too much' becomes the data harm.

Building on the acknowledgement that personal data assemblages are more-than-human phenomena that are invested with vitalities and vibrancies in emergent and complex ways, we can develop a new ethics of affinity, care and compassion towards them, similar to those espoused by feminist new materialism scholars towards the environment and nonhuman animal life, or more specifically, akin to the Japanese techno-animism concept. I argue that this care and compassion should involve the recognition and recuperation of the humanness of personal data assemblages. What if we thought of our personal data as a new form of human remains? As archaeological artefacts? Are they like our bones – or more like objects we have made through craft-work? Should we think of them as souvenirs or mementos? Or as companion species? What other ways can we think of for storing, materializing, realizing and engaging the vitalities and vibrancies of our personal data assemblages? What implications do these questions have for our moral and ethical engagements with our personal data? How can we best live with and through our data? What are the futures of our data?

The value of personal data for people's lives, and the ways they make sense of the data, involve complex interactions between embodied sensory knowledge and information that is generated from digital devices and online interactions. On the basis of these concepts, we can start to think about the ways in which these liminal human–nonhuman artefacts change over time and the social relations and material contexts in which they are generated and become objects for sense-making. We can consider how humans make and remake these digital data, and how these data make and remake humans, and where the congruences and frictions are, and how they are enacted. We can begin to explore the ways in which these correspondences are inevitably subject to rupture and how choices are made about which data are considered to be important or valuable (to resonate) and which are ignored or considered useless. The affective forces that data materializations can provoke may engender queasy feelings and, in doing so, potentially awaken people to where their data may not work, fail to fit, lose their seamless nature and create friction.

Discomfort and disquiet can become more than personal affects – they can provoke political responses. We can, perhaps, begin to think about a type of critical data politics that may be enacted via data materializations and data affects, where data simply do not 'make sense' because they do not 'feel right'. Approaches that adopt a perspective leading to responses to personal data which invite users to take up ludic, creative and improvised engagements (Gaver et al. 2013), create their own data-things (Nissen and Bowers 2015), encourage them to invest objects with even more personal and intimate features by overlaying a patina of personal data on them (Lee et al. 2016) or demonstrate to them the lively affective forces and relational connections generated by their data, as in some of the design- and arts-based approaches discussed in chapter 3, may be one way forward. These approaches provide possibilities for the generation of alternative or counter-perspectives and greater opportunities for people to 'feel' their data in ways which make sense in the context of their own lives. They can also be taken up to surface the political implications of datafication and dataveillance by identifying which actors and agencies benefit from the configuration and manipulation of data selves, while others' agencies are restricted.

Appendix

Material from several different research projects I have recently undertaken involving Australians discussing their personal data practices and understandings is included in this book. Details of these projects and the participants are provided below, as well as the project output publication details. Some parts from several of these publications are included in this book in revised and reconfigured form.

All the projects were approved by the University of Canberra's Human Research Ethics Committee and funded by personal research funds provided to me by the University of Canberra as part of the Centenary Professor appointment I held between 2014 and 2018.

Australian Women's Use of Digital Media for Pregnancy and Parenting (2015)

This project involved a survey of 410 women around Australia and four focus groups held in Sydney. The focus group discussions were designed to explore issues around the women's use of apps and other online media for pregnancy and parenting. The participants were asked to talk about the types of digital media they used for pregnancy and parenting purposes, why they used them and in what ways they found them useful or helpful (or not). Three groups included women who already had young children (a total of twenty-seven women, some of whom were pregnant at the time of the study), and the fourth comprised nine women who were pregnant for the first time. Eleven participants were aged between 23 and 29, twenty-two were aged between 30 and 39 and three were 40 years or older. They were predominantly a highly educated group. Twenty-six women held university degree qualifications. A further seven participants had technical training, and only three had high school qualifications only.

Collaborators: Sarah Pedersen collaborated on the publication from this project that reported the survey findings.

Publications: Lupton 2016c; 2017a; Lupton and Pedersen 2016.

Self-Tracking Cyclists (2015–2016)

This project investigated the experiences of cyclists who used digital self-tracking devices. In videotaped interviews the participants were asked to explain their cycling and self-tracking history and practices. Participants filmed one of their trips using a GoPro camera mounted on their cycling helmet. Once this ride was recorded, another interview took place in which the participants viewed their video while they discussed how they felt on the ride, what they were looking at or taking notice of as they rode, and whether they checked their self-tracking devices during the ride. The project involved eight people in Canberra (four women and four men) and ten in Melbourne (four women and six men). The participants ranged in age from their late twenties to their mid-fifties. All of them were in managerial or professional positions, working in occupations such as academia, the public service, engineering and IT.

Collaborators: Sarah Pink, Christine Heyes Labond and Shanti Sumartojo collaborated on all publications from this project.

Publications: Sumartojo et al. 2016; Pink et al. 2017a; 2017b; Lupton et al. 2018.

Australian Self-Trackers (2016)

For this project, forty participants from around Australia who engaged in some form of self-tracking took part in a telephone interview. The interview schedule included questions about what people were self-tracking, the methods they were using, why they took up self-tracking, what benefits they gained from it, any frustrations or disappointments they had experienced, how accurate they thought the information they gathered was, whether they shared it with anyone else and whether they had any concerns about the privacy or security of their personal data. To ensure an even gender and age spread, sub-quotas were set of twenty men and twenty women, twenty participants aged 40 or under and twenty aged over 40 (the oldest participant was aged 75). The vast majority of participants came from the states of Victoria (eighteen people) and New South Wales (nineteen people), and lived in the capital cities of those states (Sydney or Melbourne), with the others hailing from Adelaide, Brisbane or regional cities in New South Wales or Victoria. More than half held a university degree.

Collaborators: Gavin Smith collaborated on one of the publications from this project.

Publications: Lupton and Smith 2018; Lupton 2019b; 2019c.

Australian Women and Digital Health (2016–2017)

In this project, a total of sixty-six women participants across two studies were involved in either interviews or focus group discussions. They were asked to talk about the technologies they used to find, generate and share information about health and medical topics across the full range available to them (from online discussion forums and websites to the newer technologies of apps, social media and wearable devices) and which they found most useful or beneficial.

Study 1 involved three sets of women living in Canberra, totalling thirty-six participants. The first set included a total of eleven women who attended an initial community forum. Following this forum, another twelve participants (aged from 21 to 63) were recruited to take part in individual face-to-face interviews. Three further focus groups with a total of thirteen women were also conducted. Focus Group 1 included four women with young children who were part of a support group for mothers living with mental health conditions (aged from 25 to 30), Focus Group 2 comprised six women with young children (aged from 25 to 33), and Focus Group 3 included three women aged in their mid to late fifties. Twenty-two participants reported university-level education, while fourteen had high school or technical qualifications. *Study 2* involved telephone interviews with thirty women living in various locations around Australia. This group of participants were recruited using sub-quotas based on age, to ensure a good spread of ages: ten aged 18 to 40, ten aged 41 to 60, ten aged 61 and over. These participants ranged in age from 22 to 74. Two-thirds lived in major cities, one-third lived in rural or remote Australia. Twenty participants lived in the state of New South Wales, four in Queensland, five in Victoria and one in Western Australia. Of this group, fourteen reported university qualifications, and the remaining sixteen participants had high school or technical qualifications.

Collaborators: Sarah Maslen collaborated on several of the publications from this project.

Publications: Lupton 2018a; Lupton and Maslen 2018; 2019; Maslen and Lupton 2019; in press; Lupton 2019a.

Data Personas (2018)

This study gave participants the opportunity to consider the ways in which digital data are generated about them, who benefits from these data and the risks and harms of these data for themselves. It also provoked them to consider how they themselves could use the data for their own purposes, how their data could be protected and preserved for their own purposes, and what measures could be introduced in the future to help them benefit from their data. An online platform developed by a market research company that is tailored towards qualitative research was used. Questions were uploaded onto the platform and participants were asked to type in their answers, which could be viewed by myself in real time. I was able to review answers as they were uploaded by the participants, and to prompt participants to elaborate on their answers and provide clarification of questions if participants required it. A total of forty participants were involved, from all states in Australia; twenty-two women and eighteen men. The participant group was on the younger side: twenty-eight were aged 18 to 39, while twelve were aged over 40 (only two were aged 60 or over). Eighteen had high school or technical college training; the remainder (twenty-two) had university-level education.

References

Albrechtslund, A. and Lauritsen, P. (2013) 'Spaces of everyday surveillance: Unfolding an analytical concept of participation', *Geoforum*, 49: 310–16.

Allison, A. (2006) *Millennial Monsters: Japanese Toys and the Global Imagination*. Berkeley: University of California Press.

Ananny, M. and Crawford, K. (2016) 'Seeing without knowing: Limitations of the transparency ideal and its application to algorithmic accountability', *New Media & Society*, 20(3): 973–89.

Andrejevic, M. (2013) *Infoglut: How Too Much Information Is Changing the Way We Think and Know*. New York: Routledge.

Andrejevic, M. (2014) 'The big data divide', *International Journal of Communication*, 8: 1673–89.

Arnold, M., Gibbs, M., Kohn, T., Meese, J. and Nansen, B. (2017) *Death and Digital Media*. London: Routledge.

Avital, M., Mathiassen, L. and Schultze, U. (2017) 'Alternative genres in information systems research', *European Journal of Information Systems*, 26(3): 240–7.

Bannerman, S. (2018) 'Relational privacy and the networked governance of the self', *Information, Communication & Society*, https://doi.org/10.1080/1369118X.2018.1478982

Barad, K. (2003) 'Posthumanist performativity: Toward an understanding of how matter comes to matter', *Signs*, 28(3): 801–31.

Barad, K. (2007) *Meeting the Universe Halfway: Quantum Physics and the Entanglement of Matter and Meaning*. Durham, NC: Duke University Press.

Barad, K. (2014) 'Diffracting diffraction: cutting together-apart', *Parallax*, 20(3): 168–87.

Barcena, M.B., Wueest, C. and Lau, H. (2014) *How Safe Is Your Quantified Self?*, Mountain View, CA: Symantec.

Barnes, S.B. (2006) 'A privacy paradox: Social networking in the United States', *First Monday*, 11 (9), https://firstmonday.org/article/view/1394/1312_2

Bassett, D.J. (2018) 'Ctrl+Alt+Delete: The changing landscape of the uncanny valley and the fear of second loss', *Current Psychology*, https://doi.org/10.1007/s12144-018-0006-5

Beer, D. (2016) *Metric Power*. Houndmills: Palgrave Macmillan.

Beer, D. (2017) 'The social power of algorithms', *Information, Communication & Society*, 20(1): 1–13.

Bennett, J. (2001) *The Enchantment of Modern Life: Attachments, Crossings, and Ethics*. Princeton, NJ: Princeton University Press.

Bennett, J. (2004) 'The force of things: Steps toward an ecology of matter', *Political Theory*, 32(3): 347–72.

Bennett, J. (2005) 'The agency of assemblages and the North American blackout', *Public Culture*, 17(3): 445–65.

Bennett, J. (2009) *Vibrant Matter: A Political Ecology of Things*. Durham, NC: Duke University Press.

Bhavnani, K.-K. and Haraway, D. (1994) 'Shifting the subject: A conversation between Kum-Kum Bhavnani and Donna Haraway, 12 April 1993, Santa Cruz, California', *Feminism & Psychology*, 4(1): 19–39.

Blas, Z. (2018) 'Face Cages'. Available at http://www.zachblas.info/works/face-cages/

Boellstorff, T. (2013) 'Making big data, in theory', *First Monday*, 18(10), https://firstmonday.org/article/view/4869/3750

Bogost, I. (2018) 'Welcome to the age of privacy nihilism', *Atlantic*, 23 August. Available at https://www.theatlantic.com/technology/archive/2018/08/the-age-of-privacy-nihilism-is-here/568198/

Bollmer, G.D. (2013) 'Millions now living will never die: Cultural anxieties about the afterlife of information', *Information Society*, 29(3): 142–51.

Braidotti, R. (2018) 'A theoretical framework for the critical posthumanities', *Theory, Culture & Society*, https://doi.org/10.1177/0263276418771486

Brain, T. (2019) 'Smell Dating'. Available at http://smell.dating/

Brandtzaeg, P.B., Pultier, A. and Moen, G.M. (2018) 'Losing control to data-hungry apps: A mixed-methods approach to mobile app privacy', *Social Science Computer Review*, https://doi.org/10.1177/0894439318777706

Buckland, M.K. (1991) 'Information as thing', *Journal of the American Society for Information Science*, 42(5): 351–60.

Burri, R.V. (2012) 'Visual rationalities: Towards a sociology of images', *Current Sociology*, 60(1): 45–60.

Burri, R.V., Schubert, C. and Strübing, J. (2011) 'The five senses of science', *Science, Technology & Innovation Studies*, 7(1): 3–7.

Cameron, E. (2010) *Enchanted Europe: Superstition, Reason, and Religion 1250–1750*. Oxford: Oxford University Press.

Campkin, B. and Cox, R. (2012) 'Introduction: Materialities and metaphors of dirt and cleanliness', in Campkin, B. and Cox, R. (eds) *Dirt: New Geographies of Cleanliness and Contamination*. London: I.B. Tauris, pp. 1–8.

Carew, P.J. (2018) 'Symbiosis or assimilation: Critical reflections on the ontological self at the precipice of Total Data', *AI & Society*, 33(3): 357–68.

Cariou, W. (2018) 'Sweetgrass stories: Listening for animate land', *Cambridge Journal of Postcolonial Literary Inquiry*, 5(3): 338–52.

Carroll, S. (2018) 'The Internet of Things is going to need an Internet of Me', *Medium*. Available at https://medium.com/the-internet-of-me/the-internet-of-things-is-going-to-need-an-internet-of-me-a1d7ed9c0cb2

Cate, F.H. (2016) 'Big data, consent, and the future of data protection', in Sugimoto, C., Ekbia, H.R. and Mattioli, M. (eds) *Big Data Is Not a Monolith*. Cambridge, MA: MIT Press, pp. 3–19.

Cecez-Kecmanovic, D., Galliers, R.D., Henfridsson, O., Newell, S. and Vidgen, R. (2014) 'The sociomateriality of information systems: Current status, future directions', *MIS Quarterly*, 38(3): 809–30.

Chambers, D. (2013) *Social Media and Personal Relationships: Online Intimacies and Networked Friendship*. Houndmills: Palgrave Macmillan.

Chen, M.Y. (2012) *Animacies: Biopolitics, Racial Mattering, and Queer Affect*. Durham, NC: Duke University Press.

Cifor, M. (2016) 'Affecting relations: Introducing affect theory to archival discourse', *Archival Science*, 16(1): 7–31.

Cifor, M. (2017) 'Stains and remains: Liveliness, materiality, and the archival lives of queer bodies', *Australian Feminist Studies*, 32(91–92): 5–21.

Cifor, M. and Gilliland, A.J. (2016) 'Affect and the archive, archives and their affects: An introduction to the special issue', *Archival Science*, 16(1): 1–6.

Classen, C. (2012) *The Deepest Sense: A Cultural History of Touch*. Urbana, IL: University of Illinois Press.

Colebrook, C. and Weinstein, J. (2017) 'Preface: Postscript on the posthuman', in Weinstein, J. and Colebrook, C. (eds) *Posthumous Life: Theorizing beyond the Posthuman*. New York: Columbia University Press, pp. ix–xxix.

Crawford, K. and Schultz, J. (2014) 'Big data and due process: Toward a framework to redress predictive privacy harms', *Boston College Law Review*, 55(1): 93–128.

Curran, D. (2018) 'Are you ready? Here is all the data Facebook and Google have on you', *Guardian*, 30 March. Available at https://www.theguardian.com/commentisfree/2018/mar/28/all-the-data-facebook-google-has-on-you-privacy

Danaher, J. (2016) 'The threat of algocracy: Reality, resistance and accommodation', *Philosophy & Technology*, 29(3): 245–68.

Data Cuisine (2018) 'What is the taste of data?'. Available at http://data-cuisine.net/

Data Physicalization Wiki (2019). Available at http://dataphys.org/

Davis, J.L. and Chouinard, J.B. (2016) 'Theorizing affordances: From request to refuse', *Bulletin of Science, Technology & Society*, 36(4): 241–8.

de la Bellacasa, M.P. (2012) '"Nothing comes without its world": Thinking with care', *Sociological Review*, 60(2): 197–216.

DeSilvey, C. (2006) 'Observed decay: Telling stories with mutable things', *Journal of Material Culture*, 11(3): 318–38.

Dewey-Hagborg, H. (2019) 'Stranger Visions'. Available at https://deweyhagborg.com/projects/stranger-visions

D'Ignazio, C. (2015) 'What would feminist data visualization look like?', MIT Center for Civic Media. Available at https://civic.mit.edu/feminist-data-visualization

Dolphijn, R. and Van der Tuin, I. (2012) *New Materialism: Interviews & Cartographies*. Ann Arbor, MI: Open Humanities Press.

Douglas, M. (1966) *Purity and Danger: An Analysis of Concepts of Pollution and Taboo*. London: Routledge & Kegan Paul.

Dovey, M. (2019) 'Respiratory Mining'. Available at http://maxdovey.com/?page=performance&id=respiratory-mining

Dunne, A. and Raby, F. (2013) *Speculative Everything: Design, Fiction, and Social Dreaming*. Cambridge, MA: The MIT Press.

Duschinsky, R. (2013) 'The politics of purity: When, actually, is dirt matter out of place?', *Thesis Eleven*, 119(1): 63–77.

Ebeling, M. (2016) *Healthcare and Big Data: Digital Specters and Phantom Objects*. Houndmills: Palgrave Macmillan.

Elish, M.C. and boyd, d. (2018) 'Situating methods in the magic of Big Data and AI', *Communication Monographs*, 85(1): 57–80.

Elwood, S. (2008) 'Volunteered geographic information: Future research directions motivated by critical, participatory, and feminist GIS', *GeoJournal*, 72(3–4): 173–83.

Esmonde, K. and Jette, S. (2018) 'Assembling the "Fitbit subject": a Foucauldian-sociomaterialist examination of social class, gender and self-surveillance on Fitbit community message boards', *Health*, https://doi.org/10.1177/1363459318800166

Eubanks, V. (2018) *Automating Inequality: How High-Tech Tools Profile, Police, and Punish the Poor*. New York: St. Martin's Press.

European Commission (2018) '2018 reform of EU data protection rules'. Available at https://ec.europa.eu/commission/priorities/justice-and-fundamental-rights/data-protection/2018-reform-eu-data-protection-rules_en

Ferryman, K. and Winn, R.A. (2018) 'Artificial intelligence can entrench disparities – here's what we must do'. *Cancer Letter*, 16 November. Available at https://cancerletter.com/articles/20181116_1/

Floridi, L. and Taddeo, M. (2016) 'What is data ethics?', *Philosophical Transactions of the Royal Society of London A*, 374 (2083), https://doi.org/10.1098/rsta.2016.0360

Fors, V., Bäckström, Å. and Pink, S. (2013) 'Multisensory emplaced learning: Resituating situated learning in a moving world', *Mind, Culture, and Activity*, 20(2): 170–83.

Foucault, M. (1979) *The History of Sexuality: An Introduction*. London: Penguin.

Foucault, M. (2008) *The Birth of Biopolitics: Lectures at the Collège de France, 1978–79*. Houndmills: Palgrave Macmillan.

Fox, T. (2018) 'Posthuman relations'. Available at http://www.tylersfox.com/#/487/

Frank, M., Walker, J., Attard, J. and Tygel, A. (2016) 'Data literacy – What is it and how can we make it happen?', *The Journal of Community Informatics*, 12 (3). Available at http://www.ci-journal.net/index.php/ciej/article/view/1347

Franklin, S. and Haraway, D. (2017) 'Staying with the manifesto: An interview with Donna Haraway', *Theory, Culture & Society*, 34(4): 49–63.

Fredengren, C. (2018) 'Archaeological posthumanities: Feminist re-invention of science and material pasts', in Åsberg, C. and Braidotti, R. (eds) *A Feminist Companion to the Posthumanities*. Cham: Springer, pp. 129–40.

Frick, L. (2019) Laurie Frick, available at https://www.lauriefrick.com/

Frosh, P. and Becker, K. (2015) 'Visual frictions', *Journal of Aesthetics & Culture*, 7(1), 30347, https://doi.org/10.3402/jac.v7.30347

Frost, S. (2016) *Biocultural Creatures: Toward a New Theory of the Human*. Durham, NC: Duke University Press.

Fuchs, C. (2014) *Social Media: A Critical Introduction*. London: Sage.

Gaver, W.W., Bowers, J., Boehner, K., Boucher, A., Cameron, D.W.T., Hauenstein, M., Jarvis, N. and Pennington, S. (2013) 'Indoor weather stations: Investigating a ludic approach to environmental HCI through batch prototyping'. *Proceedings of the SIGCHI Conference on Human Factors in Computing Systems (CHI'13), Paris*. New York: ACM Press, pp. 3451–60.

Gehl, R.W. (2011) 'The archive and the processor: The internal logic of Web 2.0', *New Media & Society*, 13(8): 1228–44.

Geller, T. (2008) 'Overcoming the uncanny valley', *IEEE Computer Graphics and Applications*, 28(4): 11–17.

Gerlitz, C. and Helmond, A. (2013) 'The like economy: Social buttons and the data-intensive web', *New Media & Society*, 15(8): 1348–65.

Gitelman, L. and Jackson, V. (2013) 'Introduction', in Gitelman, L. (ed.) *'Raw Data' Is an Oxymoron*. Cambridge, MA: MIT Press, pp. 1–14.

Goggin, G., Vromen, A., Wetherall, K., Martin, F., Webb, A., Sunman, L. and Bailo, F. (2017) *Digital Rights in Australia*. Sydney: University of Sydney.

Goldacre, B. (2014) 'When data gets creepy: The secrets we don't realise we are giving away', *Guardian*, 5 December. Available at https://www.theguardian.com/technology/2014/dec/05/when-data-gets-creepy-secrets-were-giving-away

Gregg, M. (2015a) 'The gift that is not given', in Boellstorff, T. and Maurer, B. (eds) *Data, Now Bigger and Better!* Chicago, IL: Prickly Paradigm, pp. 47–66.

Gregg, M. (2015b) 'Inside the data spectacle', *Television & New Media*, 16(1): 37–51.

Gross, S., Bardzell, J., Bardzell, S. and Stallings, M. (2017) 'Persuasive anxiety: Designing and deploying material and formal explorations of personal tracking devices', *Human–Computer Interaction*, 32(5–6): 297–334.

Haldrup, M. (2017) 'Souvenirs: Magical objects in everyday life', *Emotion, Space and Society*, 22: 52–60.

Hallam, E. (2010) 'Articulating bones: An epilogue', *Journal of Material Culture*, 15(4): 465–92.

Hallam, E. (2016) *Anatomy Museum: Death and the Body Displayed*. London: Reaktion Books.

Hanna, C. (2018) 'Dear Apple, while we're talking about creepy data collection ...', *The Sydney Morning Herald*, 11 April. Available at https://www.smh.com.au/technology/dear-apple-while-we-re-talking-about-creepy-data-collection-20180411-p4z8wh.html

Haraway, D. (1991) *Simians, Cyborgs and Women: The Reinvention of Nature*. London: Free Association.

Haraway, D. (1995) 'Foreword: Cyborgs and symbionts: Living together in the new world order', in Gray, C.H. (ed.) *The Cyborg Handbook*. New York: Routledge, pp. xi–xx.

Haraway, D. (2003) *The Companion Species Manifesto: Dogs, People, and Significant Otherness*. Chicago, IL: Prickly Paradigm.

Haraway, D. (2015a) 'Anthropocene, capitalocene, plantationocene, chthulucene: Making kin', *Environmental Humanities*, 6(1): 159–65.

Haraway, D. (2015b) 'Birth of the kennel: A lecture by Donna Haraway, August 2000', *The European Graduate School*. Available at https://www.youtube.com/playlist?list=PL1D9615FA85ED8B19

Haraway, D. (2016) *Staying with the Trouble: Making Kin in the Chthulucene*. Durham, NC: Duke University Press.

Hargittai, E. and Marwick, A. (2016) '"What can I really do?" Explaining the privacy paradox with online apathy', *International Journal of Communication*, 10. Available at http://ijoc.org/index.php/ijoc/article/view/4655/1738

Hayles, N.K. (2008) *How We Became Posthuman: Virtual Bodies in Cybernetics, Literature, and Informatics*. Chicago, IL: University of Chicago Press.

Hayles, N.K. (2012) *How We Think: Digital Media and Contemporary Technogenesis*. Chicago, IL: University of Chicago Press.

Hill, R.L., Kennedy, H. and Gerrard, Y. (2016) 'Visualizing junk: Big data visualizations and the need for feminist data studies', *Journal of Communication Inquiry*, 40(4): 331–50.

Hintz, A., Dencik, L. and Wahl-Jorgensen, K. (2019) *Digital Citizenship in a Datafied Society*. Cambridge: Polity.

Hogan, M. (2018) 'Big data ecologies', *Ephemera*, 18(3): 631–57.

Hornborg, A. (2006) 'Animism, fetishism, and objectivism as strategies for knowing (or not knowing) the world', *Ethnos*, 71(1): 21–32.

Hultman, K. and Lenz Taguchi, H. (2010) 'Challenging anthropocentric analysis of visual data: A relational materialist methodological approach to educational research', *International Journal of Qualitative Studies in Education*, 23(5): 525–42.

Ingold, T. (2011) *Being Alive: Essays on Movement, Knowledge and Description*. London: Taylor & Francis.

Ingold, T. (2013) *Making: Anthropology, Archaeology, Art and Architecture*. London: Routledge.

Ingold, T. and Hallam, E. (2014) 'Making and growing: An introduction', in Ingold, T. and Hallam, E. (eds) *Making and Growing: Anthropological Studies of Organisms and Artefacts*. London: Routledge, pp. 1–24.

Institute of Human Obsolescence (2019). Available at http://speculative.capital

Jansen, Y., Dragicevic, P., Isenberg, P., Alexander, J., Karnik, A., Kildal, J., Subramanian, S. and Hornbæk, K. (2015) 'Opportunities and challenges for data physicalization'. *Proceedings of the 33rd Annual ACM Conference on Human Factors in Computing Systems, Seoul*. New York: ACM, pp. 3227–36.

Jasanoff, S. (2015) 'Future imperfect: Science, technology, and the imaginations of modernity', in Jasanoff, S. and Kim, S.-H. (eds)

Dreamscapes of Modernity: Sociotechnical Imaginaries and the Fabrication of Power. Chicago, IL: University of Chicago Press, pp. 1–33.

Jay, M. (2002) 'Cultural relativism and the visual turn', *Journal of Visual Culture*, 1(3): 267–78.

Jensen, C.B. and Blok, A. (2013) 'Techno-animism in Japan: Shinto cosmograms, actor-network theory, and the enabling powers of non-human agencies', *Theory, Culture & Society*, 30(2): 84–115.

John, N. (2017) *The Age of Sharing.* Cambridge: Polity.

Jones, A. and Hoskins, T.K. (2016) 'A mark on paper: The matter of indigenous-settler history', in Taylor, C.A. and Hughes, C. (eds) *Posthuman Research Practices in Education.* Houndmills: Palgrave Macmillan, pp. 75–92.

Jones, A.M. and Alberti, B. (2016) 'Archaeology and interpretation', in Alberti, B., Jones, A.M. and Pollard, J. (eds) *Archaeology After Interpretation: Returning Materials to Archaeological Theory.* London: Routledge, pp. 15–35.

Kember, S. and Zylinska, J. (2012) *Life after New Media: Mediation as a Vital Process.* Cambridge, MA: MIT Press.

Kennedy, H. (2016) *Post, Mine, Repeat: Social Media Data Mining Becomes Ordinary.* London: Palgrave Macmillan.

Kennedy, H., Elgesem, D. and Miguel, C. (2017) 'On fairness: User perspectives on social media data mining', *Convergence*, 23(3): 270–88.

Kennedy, H. and Hill, R.L. (2017) 'The pleasure and pain of visualizing data in times of data power', *Television & New Media*, 18(8): 769–82.

Kennedy, H. and Hill, R.L. (2018) 'The feeling of numbers: Emotions in everyday engagements with data and their visualisation', *Sociology*, 52(4): 830–48.

Kennedy, H., Hill, R.L., Allen, W. and Aiello, G. (2016) 'The work that visualisation conventions do', *Information, Communication & Society*, 19(6): 715–35.

Kennedy, H. and Moss, G. (2015) 'Known or knowing publics? Social media data mining and the question of public agency', *Big Data & Society*, 2 (2), https://doi.org/10.1177/2053951715611145

Kitchin, R. (2014) *The Data Revolution: Big Data, Open Data, Data Infrastructures and Their Consequences.* London: Sage.

Kleinman, A. (2018) 'Intra-actions', *Mousse*, 34: 76–81.

Kokolakis, S. (2017) 'Privacy attitudes and privacy behaviour: A review of current research on the privacy paradox phenomenon', *Computers & Security*, 64: 122–34.

Koro-Ljungberg, M., Löytönen, T. and Tesar, M. (2017) 'Introduction: Multiplicities of data encounters', in Koro-Ljungberg,

M., Löytönen, T. and Tesar, M. (eds) *Disrupting Data in Qualitative Inquiry: Entanglements with the Post-Critical and Post-Anthropocentric*. New York: Peter Lang, pp. 1–9.

Kristeva, J. (1982) *Powers of Horror: An Essay on Abjection*. New York: Columbia University Press.

Kuntsman, A. (2012) 'Introduction: Affective fabrics of digital cultures', in Karatzogianni, A. and Kuntsman, A. (eds) *Digital Cultures and the Politics of Emotion: Feelings, Affect and Technological Change*. Houndmills: Palgrave Macmillan, pp. 1–17.

Kwan, M.-P. (2002) 'Feminist visualization: Re-envisioning GIS as a method in feminist geographic research', *Annals of the Association of American Geographers*, 92(4): 645–61.

Lagerkvist, A. (2017) 'Existential media: Toward a theorization of digital thrownness', *New Media & Society*, 19(1): 96–110.

Lambert, A. (2013) *Intimacy and Friendship on Facebook*. Houndmills: Palgrave Macmillan.

Lather, P. and St. Pierre, E.A. (2013) 'Post-qualitative research', *International Journal of Qualitative Studies in Education*, 26(6): 629–33.

Latimer, J. (2008) 'Introduction: body, knowledge, worlds', *The Sociological Review*, 56(2 Suppl.): 1–22.

Latour, B. (1986) 'Visualization and cognition', *Knowledge and Society*, 6(1): 1–40.

Latour, B. (1993) *We Have Never Been Modern*. New York: Harvester Wheatsheaf.

Leaver, T. (2017) 'Intimate surveillance: Normalizing parental monitoring and mediation of infants online', *Social Media + Society*, 3 (2), http://dx.doi.org/10.1177/2056305117707192

Lee, J.A. (2016) 'Be/longing in the archival body: Eros and the "Endearing" value of material lives', *Archival Science*, 16(1): 33–51.

Lee, M.-H., Son, O. and Nam, T.-J. (2016) 'Patina-inspired personalization: Personalizing products with traces of daily use'. *Proceedings of the 2016 ACM Conference on Designing Interactive Systems (DIS'16), Brisbane*. New York: ACM Press, pp. 251–63.

Lenz Taguchi, H. (2012) 'A diffractive and Deleuzian approach to analysing interview data', *Feminist Theory*, 13(3): 265–81.

Leszczynski, A. (2015) 'Spatial big data and anxieties of control', *Environment and Planning D: Society and Space*, 33(6): 965–84.

Levy, K. (2015) 'Intimate surveillance', *Idaho Law Review*, 51: 679–93.

Light, A., Markham, A. and O'Connor, M. (2018) 'Glitch

memory: Raising ethical questions', *Future Making*. Available at https://futuremaking.space/morm/morm-aie-conference-2018/aie_conference_sketch/

Lupton, D. (1994) 'Panic computing: The viral metaphor and computer technology', *Cultural Studies*, 8(3): 556–68.

Lupton, D. (1995) 'The embodied computer/user', *Body & Society*, 1(3–4): 97–112.

Lupton, D. (2014) 'The commodification of patient opinion: The digital patient experience economy in the age of big data', *Sociology of Health & Illness*, 36(6): 856–69.

Lupton, D. (2015a) *Digital Sociology*. London: Routledge.

Lupton, D. (2015b) 'Quantified sex: A critical analysis of sexual and reproductive self-tracking using apps', *Culture, Health & Sexuality*, 17(4): 440–53.

Lupton, D. (2016a) 'The diverse domains of quantified selves: Self-tracking modes and dataveillance', *Economy and Society*, 45(1): 101–22.

Lupton, D. (2016b) *The Quantified Self: A Sociology of Self-Tracking*. Cambridge: Polity.

Lupton, D. (2016c) 'The use and value of digital media for information about pregnancy and early motherhood: A focus group study', *BMC Pregnancy and Childbirth*, 16(1): 171. Available at http://bmcpregnancychildbirth.biomedcentral.com/articles/10.1186/s12884-016-0971-3

Lupton, D. (2017a) '"It just gives me a bit of peace of mind": Australian women's use of digital media for pregnancy and early motherhood', *Societies*, 7(3): 25. Available at http://www.mdpi.com/2075-4698/7/3/25

Lupton, D. (2017b) 'Personal data practices in the age of lively data', in Daniels, J., Gregory, K. and McMillan Cottom, T. (eds) *Digital Sociologies*. Bristol: Policy Press, pp. 339–54.

Lupton, D. (2018a) '"I just want it to be done, done, done!" Food tracking apps, affects, and agential capacities', *Multimodal Technologies and Interaction*, 2(2): 29. Available at http://www.mdpi.com/2414-4088/2/2/29/htm

Lupton, D. (2018b) 'Lively data, social fitness and biovalue: The intersections of health self-tracking and social media', in Burgess, J., Marwick, A. and Poell, T. (eds) *The Sage Handbook of Social Media*. London: Sage, pp. 562–78.

Lupton, D. (2018c) 'Towards design sociology', *Sociology Compass*, 12(1), https://doi.org/10.1111/soc4.12546

Lupton, D. (2019a) 'The Australian Women and Digital Health Project: Comprehensive report of findings'. Available at https://apo.org.au/node/220326

Lupton, D. (2019b) '"It's made me a lot more aware": A feminist new materialist analysis of health self-tracking', *Media International Australia*, https://doi.org/10.1177/1329878X19844042.

Lupton, D. (2019c) 'Vital materialism and the thing-power of lively digital data', in Leahy, D., Fitzpatrick, K. and Wright, J. (eds) *Social Theory, Health and Education*. London: Routledge.

Lupton, D. (2019d) 'Vitalities and visceralities: Alternative body/food politics in new digital media', in Phillipov, M. and Kirkwood, K. (eds) *Alternative Food Politics: From the Margins to the Mainstream*. London: Routledge, pp. 151–68.

Lupton, D. and Maslen, S. (2018) 'The more-than-human sensorium: Sensory engagements with digital self-tracking technologies', *The Senses and Society*, 13(2): 190–202.

Lupton, D. and Maslen, S. (2019) 'How women use digital technologies for health: Qualitative interview and focus group study', *Journal of Medical Internet Research*, 21(1): e11481. Available at http://www.jmir.org/2019/1/e11481/

Lupton, D. and Michael, M. (2017) '"Depends on who's got the data": Public understandings of personal digital dataveillance', *Surveillance & Society*, 15(2): 254–68.

Lupton, D. and Pedersen, S. (2016) 'An Australian survey of women's use of pregnancy and parenting apps', *Women and Birth*, 29(4): 368–74.

Lupton, D., Pink, S., LaBond, C.H. and Sumartojo, S. (2018) 'Personal data contexts, data sense and self-tracking cycling', *International Journal of Communication*, 12. Available at http://ijoc.org/index.php/ijoc/article/view/5925/2268

Lupton, D. and Smith, G.J.D. (2018) '"A much better person": The agential capacities of self-tracking practices', in Ajana, B. (ed.) *Metric Culture: Ontologies of Self-Tracking Practices*. London: Emerald Publishing, pp. 57–73.

McCosker, A. and Wilken, R. (2014) 'Rethinking "big data" as visual knowledge: The sublime and the diagrammatic in data visualisation', *Visual Studies*, 29(2): 155–64.

MacLure, M. (2013) 'Researching without representation? Language and materiality in post-qualitative methodology', *International Journal of Qualitative Studies in Education*, 26(6): 658–67.

Marenko, B. (2014) 'Neo-animism and design: A new paradigm in object theory', *Design and Culture*, 6(2): 219–41.

Marenko, B. and van Allen, P. (2016) 'Animistic design: How to reimagine digital interaction between the human and the nonhuman', *Digital Creativity*, 27(1): 52–70.

Marwick, A. and boyd, d. (2014) 'Networked privacy: How teenagers negotiate context in social media', *New Media & Society*, 17(7): 1051–67.

Maslen, S. and Lupton, D. (2018) '"You can explore it more

online": A qualitative study on Australian women's use of online health and medical information', *BMC Health Services Research*, 18(1): 916, https://doi.org/10.1186/s12913-018-3749-7

Maslen, S. and Lupton, D. (2019) 'Enacting chronic illness with and through digital media: a feminist new materialist approach', *Information, Communication and Society*, https://doi.org/10.1080/1369118X.2019.1602665

Mele, C. (2018) 'Data breaches keep happening. So why don't you do something?', *New York Times*, 1 August, https://www.nytimes.com/2018/08/01/technology/data-breaches.html

Merleau-Ponty, M. (1962) *Phenomenology of Perception*. London: Routledge & Kegan Paul.

Merleau-Ponty, M. (1968) *The Visible and the Invisible*. Evanston, IL: Nortwestern University Press.

Miller, J. (2018) 'Conflict Sculptures'. Available at https://www.jillmiller.net/#/conflictsculptures/

Mittelstadt, B.D. and Floridi, L. (2016) 'The ethics of big data: Current and foreseeable issues in biomedical contexts', in Mittelstadt, B.D. and Floridi, L. (eds) *The Ethics of Biomedical Big Data*. Cham: Springer International Publishing, pp. 445–80.

Mori, M., MacDorman, K.F. and Kageki, N. (2012) 'The uncanny valley', *IEEE Robotics & Automation Magazine*, 19(2): 98–100.

Morone, J.L. (2018) 'Jennifer Lyn Morone, Inc'. Available at http://jenniferlynmorone.com/

Munn, L. (2019) 'Domestic Data'. Available at http://www.lukemunn.com/2017/domestic-data/

Neubarth, M. (2013) 'Data hygiene: Create a culture of cleanliness to beat bad data', *Towerd@ta*, 10 July. Available at https://www.towerdata.com/blog/bid/116955/data-hygiene-create-a-culture-of-cleanliness-to-beat-bad-data

Nissen, B. and Bowers, J. (2015) 'Data-things: Digital fabrication situated within participatory data translation activities'. *Proceedings of the 33rd Annual ACM Conference on Human Factors in Computing Systems (CHI'15), Seoul*. New York: ACM, pp. 2467–76.

Nissenbaum, H. (2011) 'A contextual approach to privacy online', *Daedalus*, 140(4): 32–48.

Niva, M. (2017) 'Online weight-loss services and a calculative practice of slimming', *Health*, 21(4): 409–24.

Noble, S.U. (2018) *Algorithms of Oppression: How Search Engines Reinforce Racism*. New York: NYU Press.

Nuffield Council on Bioethics (2015) *The Collection, Linking and Use of Data in Biomedical Research and Health Care: Ethical Issues*. London: Nuffield Council on Bioethics.

Obar, J.A. (2015) 'Big data and the phantom public: Walter Lippmann and the fallacy of data privacy self-management', *Big Data & Society*, 2(2), https://doi.org/10.1177/2053951715608876

O'Connor, M., Markham, A. and Pereira, G. (2018) 'The un-archivable and the sound of forgetting', *Future Making*. Available at https://futuremaking.space/morm/data-justice/the-un-archivable/

Öhman, C. and Floridi, L. (2018) 'An ethical framework for the digital afterlife industry', *Nature Human Behaviour*, 2(5): 318–20.

O'Neil, C. (2016) *Weapons of Math Destruction: How Big Data Increases Inequality and Threatens Democracy*. London: Penguin.

Orlikowski, W.J. and Scott, S.V. (2008) 'Sociomateriality: Challenging the separation of technology, work and organization', *Academy of Management Annals*, 2(1): 433–74.

Orlikowski, W.J. and Scott, S.V. (2015) 'Exploring material-discursive practices', *Journal of Management Studies*, 52(5): 697–705.

panGenerator (2019) 'hash2hash – Everything saved will be lost'. Available at https://vimeo.com/254393034

Parikka, J. (2012) 'New materialism as media theory: Medianatures and dirty matter', *Communication and Critical/Cultural Studies*, 9(1): 95–100.

Pasquale, F. (2015) *The Black Box Society: The Secret Algorithms that Control Money and Information*. Boston, MA: Harvard University Press.

Paterson, M. (2007) *The Senses of Touch: Haptics, Affects and Technologies*. Oxford: Berg.

Pavlovskaya, M. (2006) 'Theorizing with GIS: A tool for critical geographies?', *Environment and Planning A*, 38(11): 2003–20.

Pentzold, C., Brantner, C. and Fölsche, L. (2019) 'Imagining big data: Illustrations of "big data" in US news articles, 2010–2016', *New Media & Society*, 21(1): 139–67.

Pink, S. and Fors, V. (2017) 'Being in a mediated world: Self-tracking and the mind–body–environment', *Cultural Geographies*, 24(3): 375–88.

Pink, S., Sumartojo, S., Lupton, D. and Heyes LaBond, C. (2017a) 'Empathetic technologies: Digital materiality and video ethnography', *Visual Studies*, 32(4): 371–81.

Pink, S., Sumartojo, S., Lupton, D. and Heyes LaBond, C. (2017b) 'Mundane data: The routines, contingencies and accomplishments of digital living', *Big Data & Society*, 4(1), http://dx.doi.org/10.1177/2053951717700924

Quan-Haase, A. and Elueze, I. (2018) 'Revisiting the privacy paradox: Concerns and protection strategies in the social media experiences of older adults'. *Proceedings of the 9th International Conference on Social Media and Society, Copenhagen*. New York: ACM, pp. 150–9.

Raley, R. (2013) 'Dataveillance and countervailance', in Gitelman, L. (ed.) *'Raw Data' Is an Oxymoron*. Cambridge, MA: MIT Press, 121–45.

Ramsay, N. (2009) 'Taking-place: Refracted enchantment and the habitual spaces of the tourist souvenir', *Social & Cultural Geography*, 10(2): 197–217.

Räsänen, M. and Nyce, J.M. (2013) 'The raw is cooked: Data in intelligence practice', *Science, Technology & Human Values*, 38(5): 655–77.

Ravenscroft, A. (2018) 'Strange weather: Indigenous materialisms, new materialism, and colonialism', *Cambridge Journal of Postcolonial Literary Inquiry*, 5(3): 353–70.

Raynes-Goldie, K. (2010) 'Aliases, creeping, and wall cleaning: Understanding privacy in the age of Facebook', *First Monday*, 15(1). Available at https://firstmonday.org/article/view/2775/2432

Redden, J. and Brand, J. (2019) 'Data harm record'. Available at https://datajusticelab.org/data-harm-record/

Rose, D. (2014) *Enchanted Objects: Design, Human Desire, and the Internet of Things*. New York: Scribner.

Rosenblat, A., Wikelius, K., boyd, d., Gangadharan, S.P. and Yu, C. (2014) 'Data & civil rights: Health primer', Data & Society Research Institute. Available at http://www.datacivilrights.org/pubs/2014-1030/Health.pdf

Rosenzweig, P. (2012) 'Whither privacy?', *Surveillance & Society*, 10(3–4): 344–7.

Sadowski, J. (2019) 'When data is capital: Datafication, accumulation, and extraction', *Big Data & Society*, 6(1), https://doi.org/10.1177/2053951718820549

St Pierre, E.A. (2013) 'Post qualitative research', in Denzin, N. and Lincoln, Y.S. (eds) *Collecting and Interpreting Qualitative Materials*. Los Angeles, CA: Sage, pp. 611–35.

Salinas, S. and Meredith, S. (2018) 'Tim Cook: Personal data collection is being "weaponized against us with military efficiency"', *CNBC*. Available at https://www.cnbc.com/2018/10/24/apples-tim-cook-warns-silicon-valley-it-would-be-destructive-to-block-strong-privacy-laws.html

Sarasohn-Kahn, J. (2014) 'Here's looking at you: How personal health information is being tracked and used'. Available at https://www.chcf.org/publication/heres-looking-at-you-how-personal-health-information-is-being-tracked-and-used/

Shove, E. (2004) *Comfort, Cleanliness and Convenience: The Social Organization of Normality*. Oxford: Berg.

Smith, A. (2018) 'Franken-algorithms: The deadly consequences of unpredictable code', *Guardian*, 30 August. Available at https://www.theguardian.com/technology/2018/aug/29/coding-algorithms-frankenalgos-program-danger

Smith, W.R. and Treem, J. (2017) 'Striving to be king of mobile mountains: Communication and organizing through digital fitness technology', *Communication Studies*, 68(2): 135–51.

Stark, L. (2016) 'The emotional context of information privacy', *The Information Society*, 32(1): 14–27.

Stephens-Davidowitz, S. (2017) *Everybody Lies: What the Internet Can Tell Us About Who We Really Are.* New York: Bloomsbury.

Stokes, P. (2015) 'Deletion as second death: The moral status of digital remains', *Ethics and Information Technology*, 17(4): 237–48.

Stragier, J., Evens, T. and Mechant, P. (2015) 'Broadcast yourself: An exploratory study of sharing physical activity on social networking sites', *Media International Australia*, 155(1): 120–9.

Strava (2019) 'Features for athletes, made by athletes'. Available at https://www.strava.com/features

Stusak, S. (2015) 'Exploring the potential of physical visualizations'. *Proceedings of the Ninth International Conference on Tangible, Embedded, and Embodied Interaction (TEI'15), Stanford, CA.* New York: ACM Press, pp. 437–40.

Sujon, Z. (2018) 'The triumph of social privacy: Understanding the privacy logics of sharing behaviors across social media', *International Journal of Communication*, 12. Available at http://ijoc.org/index.php/ijoc/article/view/9357

Sumartojo, S., Pink, S., Lupton, D. and LaBond, C.H. (2016) 'The affective intensities of datafied space', *Emotion, Space and Society*, 21: 33–40.

Szerszynski, B. (2008) *Nature, Technology and the Sacred.* London: John Wiley & Sons.

Tatham, H. (2018) 'Coding and confectionary combine to give chocolate lovers a true taste of Sydney', *ABC News*. Available at https://www.abc.net.au/news/2018-07-28/census-data-coded-chocolate-true-taste-of-sydney-ancestry/10044512

Taylor, C., Fairchild, N., Elmenhorst, C., Koro-Ljungberg, M., Benozzo, A. and Carey, N. (2018) 'Improvising bags choreographies: Disturbing normative ways of doing research', *Qualitative Inquiry*, 25(1): 17–25.

Tene, O. and Polonetsky, J. (2013a) 'Big data for all: Privacy and user control in the age of analytics', *Northwestern Journal of Technology & Intellectual Property*, 11(5): 239–73.

Tene, O. and Polonetsky, J. (2013b) 'A theory of creepy: Technology, privacy and shifting social norms', *Yale Journal of Law & Technology*, 16: 59–102.

Thrift, N. (2014) 'The "sentient" city and what it may portend', *Big Data & Society*, 1(1). Available at http://bds.sagepub.com/content/1/1/2053951714532241.full.pdf+html

Timmermans, J., Stahl, B.C., Ikonen, V. and Bozdag, E. (2010) 'The ethics of cloud computing: A conceptual review'. 2010 IEEE Second International Conference on Cloud Computing Technology and Science, Indianapolis. IEEE, pp. 614–20.

Ulguim, P. (2018) 'Digital remains made public: Sharing the dead online and our future digital mortuary landscape', *AP: Online Journal in Public Archeology*, 8(2), http://dx.doi.org/10.23914/ap.v8i2.162

van Dijck, J. (2013) *The Culture of Connectivity: A Critical History of Social Media*. Oxford: Oxford University Press.

van Dijck, J. (2014) 'Datafication, dataism and dataveillance: Big Data between scientific paradigm and ideology', *Surveillance & Society*, 12(2): 197–208.

Walter, M. (2018) 'The voice of Indigenous data: Beyond the markers of disadvantage'. Available at https://croakey.org/the-voice-of-indigenous-data-beyond-the-markers-of-disadvantage/

Weinstein, J. and Colebrook, C. (2017) 'Introduction: Critical life studies and the problems of inhuman rites and posthumous life', in Weinstein, J. and Colebrook, C. (eds) *Posthumous Life: Theorizing Beyond the Posthuman*. New York: Columbia University Press, pp. 1–14.

Wieringa, M. (2018) 'Making sense of the data-driven: SETUP's Algorithmic History Museum and its relevance for contemporary reflection', *Tijdschrift voor Mediageschiedenis*, 21(2): 187–94.

Wired Insider (2018) 'The Internet of Me: When the consumer becomes the electronics', *Wired*. Available at https://www.wired.com/brandlab/2018/01/internet-consumer-becomes-electronics

Wolff, A., Gooch, D., Cavero Montaner, J.J., Rashid, U. and Kortuem, G. (2016) 'Creating an understanding of data literacy for a data-driven society', *Journal of Community Informatics*, 12(3): 9–26.

World Economic Forum (2011) *Personal Data: The Emergence of a New Asset Class*. Geneva: World Economic Forum.

Yoo, Y. (2010) 'Computing in everyday life: A call for research on experiential computing', *MIS Quarterly*, 34(2): 213–31.

Ziebland, S. and Wyke, S. (2012) 'Health and illness in a connected world: How might sharing experiences on the internet affect people's health?', *Milbank Quarterly*, 90(2): 219–49.

Zuboff, S. (2015) 'Big other: Surveillance capitalism and the prospects of an information civilization', *Journal of Information Technology*, 30(1): 75–89.

Zwitter, A. (2014) 'Big Data ethics', *Big Data & Society*, 1(2), https://doi.org/10.1177/2053951714559253

Index